T0158991

Two Days after Christmas

Christmas

Weeping with Rachel

Lynn Payne

"A voice was heard in Ramah,
Lamentation, weeping, and great mourning,
Rachel weeping for her children,
Refusing to be comforted,
Because they are no more."
(Matthew 2:18)

First I want to dedicate this book to Jacob our angel. You will always be our shinning star. I pray that through this book your life and even your untimely death continues to touch lives. To Blake and Leslie my surviving children You have been the reason I could be happy again. Your Daddy and I are so proud of you both and I know Jacob is cheering You on from Heaven.

To Jeff my beloved husband. I could have not made it through this life without You and obviously not through the loss of our Son. You have been my one constant, my safe place and my passion. You have made all my dreams come true. I am glad we did not lose each other in this tragedy. I am thankful we loved each other through to better days.

Lastly to my God. You have trusted me with a great pain. You have blessed me immeasurably. I will serve You all my days and praise You with my last breath until we meet face to face and You shall wipe away every tear from my eye. I know Jacob will be there too. What a day that will be!

Acknowledgment

To June Saunders my writing assistant, my listener, my encourager, my friend. I truly could not have written this book without out You... your wisdom, experience empathy and patience have been vital to me in this labor of love. I will forever be grateful. To God be the Glory. I know this book will bless many lives. Thanks again from the bottom of my heart. May the Lord bless You and keep You.

Preface

Like most children, I did not realize how lucky I was. Looking back, I now consider being born into a family with a rich Christian heritage as well as monetary success to be the greatest of blessings. I was given much, and I am grateful.

All that I was given stood me in good stead when the most precious, my greatest of blessings, was taken from me. My youngest child, Jacob, died when he was just five years old.

When you've been taught things of the spirit all your life, it seems like all those teachings just kick in when such a moment strikes. I remain thankful for my Pentecostal roots because all that I was taught about the Holy Spirit came to me when I needed it the most. Maybe that wasn't a focus in your background, or maybe you find yourself a backslider in faith. If so, I understand. If you have received Jesus as your savior, though, the Holy Spirit lives in you. Because Jesus died on the cross, He sent the Holy Spirit to live in us to be our comforter and guide—to be the power in us to overcome our weaknesses and to help us to be bold.

I didn't even realize the significance of the Holy Spirit in my situation until I started looking back at how things happened. As I was writing this book, I referred to it as my "Holy Spirit Memoir." A memoir . . . it sounds so intimate and romantic. But writing about the most awful time of my life and reliving the experiences with every word was very hard. Though difficult, I still feel compelled to try to share how God helped me. He was there for me every step of the way, from the first moments I heard about the tragedy that was to befall us, all the way through to the healing and restoration of my family. I feel this is a beautiful memoir indeed—not just of how I survived the loss of my child, but the story of how my family and I are now thriving together. That is the miracle.

The Comforter is there for everyone in the same way, regardless of what you have to face. There's no magic formula I decided to apply. It has just happened this way. I would ask for His help because I knew I couldn't face the day otherwise—and I would receive that help.

As I share my story, I will do all I can to help you know this comfort too, if you do not already know it. No sorrow, no loss is too great for Him to restore. I pray above all that you can be touched by the grace of the Holy Spirit. I hope that you will come to know that even when human beings are in the deepest despair and darkness, there is love, hope, and light available from Him.

Introduction

My father and his brother owned a timber company. My daddy was strict as well as smart, hard-working and a very successful businessman. Yet church took up the bulk of his devotion. He and his brother started a Pentecostal church in our area when I was about five years old. Church was a vital part of our lives in every way. There I was, a piece of tender clay being molded by genuine Christian believers. I embraced it with a childlike faith, but the seeds for a more mature faith were being sown.

My wonderful childhood experiences were shaping my desire and passion for the things of God. A foundation was being laid that would later see me through the worst nightmare a parent can experience. We've all heard that to lose a child is the worst pain possible. Parents who have lost children explain that there is something terribly unnatural about burying your own child and living on while your child's youth and promise fade away from this earth. It seems so unfair.

There's a guilt feeling that you have outlived your own child. Almost everyone who experiences a death feels some guilt about it. Parents who lose children feel a form of survivor's guilt. They wonder, "Why was my child taken from the earth before I was? Why was he or she not allowed to have the years of life I have been given?" Even worse is the feeling, "If I had done things differently, maybe my child would still be alive."

Then there is the envy; seeing other parents enjoying their time with their living, breathing children. Just having life for a child is such a great gift, let alone being able to enjoy the life of that child alongside him or her. I remember sitting in church after Jacob's death and seeing the young children in all their Easter finery—bonnets, spring dresses, and white shoes for the girls; cunning little suits, knee socks, and new shoes for the boys. I felt pain that I had no young child for whom to buy new spring clothes. I had no big-eyed five-year-old for whom to organize an Easter egg hunt.

My other children were great comforts to me, but they were in their teens when it happened. Jacob's childhood and my delighted participation in it were over. Of course, I have had the joy of celebrating my older children's graduations and other milestones in their lives. Yet such milestones always carried the tang of sorrow; they were also markers of what could have been in the future had Jacob lived.

If you have suffered a loss, you know what I mean. For a time—sometimes for a long time—celebrations can touch the sore wounds of sorrow. To lose a child is the grief that keeps on giving on every birthday, every holiday, every marker and milestone that would have happened in their growing lives. It is pain beyond imagination.

For example, when my daughter Leslie graduated from Trinity, I thought of the Book of Ruth in the Bible. I felt like Naomi, Ruth's mother-in-law, who lost a husband and two sons. Naomi confesses that she is bitter and not joyful anymore (Ruth 1:20-21): "But she said to them, "Do not call me Naomi; call me Mara, for the Almighty has dealt very bitterly with me. I went out full, and the LORD has brought me home again empty. Why do you call me Naomi, since the LORD has testified against me, and the Almighty has afflicted me?"

Instead of "Naomi," which means "pleasantness," Naomi wanted to call herself "Mara," which means "bitter." Like Naomi, I sat there at Leslie's high school graduation and could not help but reflect on all the bitter losses of the past five years. My son Jacob had died at just five years of age; my best friend, Tammie Foster, lost her sixteen-year-old daughter, Kelly, in a car accident. Along with dealing with those losses, my sister-in–law, Rebecca, had passed after battling cancer. Leslie had struggled all through high school. My oldest son, Blake, dropped out of college twice and was running from his pain by living the prodigal life. As if all that were not enough, my husband lost his business in 2006 and we were crippled with debt. All celebrations seemed hollow. Most painful of all was the sorrow of knowing that I should have had a son in fifth grade as I celebrated Leslie's high school commencement.

You can try and be strong after one loss, but when they just keep on coming, it is hard not to grow bitter and feel empty, like Naomi. Believe me, I know. Yet Naomi's life was not empty. She had her wonderful daughter-in-law Ruth, and together they would forge a new life. A miracle was on the way.

My life was not empty either. I knew even then that there is always something to be thankful for. Time would bring miracles my way too, but I had to get past my bitterness and trust God and work with what I had.

I love it when the Book of Ruth takes a turn for the better. We see Naomi get excited about the new relationship between Ruth and Boaz and about her own life and future. She experienced great joy, I am sure, when a new generation was born in her grandson Obed, and she could feel hope for her lineage again. Maybe she had some premonition of the greatness that was to come! As it turned out, Ruth and Boaz were the great-grandparents of King David. They were also the ancestors of Jesus because Matthew tells us that Jesus was of the House of David. Since Naomi was Boaz's kinswoman, she too was related to Jesus Christ.

A reversal came for me too, after many years of sorrow. The wounds got better. You do heal. Memories of sorrow turn into memories of joy.

Jacob's high school graduation would have been the spring of 2016. Since I was invited to go, I did. It was truly beautiful. The Lord made it perfect. Blake was living in Knoxville, Tennessee, and he thought he wasn't going to be able to come, but he worked it out and was able to attend. When he called me to let me know he was coming after all, I was so thrilled. It was such good news.

"I am coming to your house!" shouted my little granddaughter Anslee over the phone. I held Anslee on my knee during the ceremony. I was back at the school for closure and realized something deep. I may have left empty when Leslie graduated and my loss of Jacob was fresh, but I came back full, like when Naomi held her grandson Obed on her knee. The one thing I desired so intently after Jacob's death was a child to love and hold—a grandchild I could love as my own. Anyone who knows of my relationship with Anslee knows she is the apple of my eye, and that we are very close. She has Jacob's personality. She has brought our whole family much joy.

Leslie and her fiancé, whom we love like a son, attended the graduation ceremony as well. They have married since and are very happy. She is starting college again this quarter and plans to be a nurse, a lifelong dream for her.

Blake is now preaching, and he and his wife are very blessed. I had dreamed of Jacob being a preacher, and that dream has become manifest through Blake's life. It is as if all the blessings of Jacob's life have still been given to us, just in different ways. I know all this would never have happened if we hadn't lost Jacob.

At the ceremony, we were a group of seven. Seven is the number for completion, for blessing. I sat among friends and family members and felt very special. In fact, I almost felt like I had a date with Jacob that day for his high school graduation—a date for which I dressed up and made myself ready so we could be proud of one another.

I had prayed for some sort of sign from him during the ceremony, but there was nothing.

As they threw up their graduation caps, I thought it was the last chance for some sign from Jacob. As I looked at all the caps flying upward, there was still nothing. Then after the ceremony, my dear friend Amy, who is the wife of my husband's best friend, came up to me.

She said, "I have something for you before you leave."

I just said, "Okay,"

Well, when we got outside she came over and handed me Jacob's old Spider Man beach towel. The best part about that was that I'd been taking that towel on vacation every year since Jacob had died, until I had lost it. The previous summer I had left it in the dryer where we were staying. I had tried to get Jeff to turn the car around so we could go back and get it, but he wouldn't. He said the towel was all worn out anyway. We were on vacation with Amy and Mitch, although they left before we did. Amy ended up with the towel and remembered it belonged to Jacob.

Well, there it was—my sign! It was like a little private smile I shared with the Lord—and with Jacob.

I felt I like I was living the full Book of Ruth. I had left that school empty but I came back full. These ancient biblical stories help us get through our very human situations with God, just as the people in the Bible did. He will bless us too, if we come through our difficulties with the faith and virtue the biblical people had. All things come to those who wait patiently on the Lord. Not only does the Lord give back what the devil stole; He will give back more if we live according to the Spirit rather than the flesh (Romans 8).

There comes a time when we celebrate again, and the bitter memories turn to ones of joy. We know laughter, family, and fellowship once again. That miracle can and will happen to you after your loss. It happened to me.

I know that if you have experienced the loss of your child or any other deep loss, you feel as if you have been violated in your very soul. You feel as if you have been robbed or even raped. Maybe some of the readers of this book know that feeling of violation deep inside; the feeling that something has been ripped out of your life and you are left raw, aching, and empty. You feel like you will never be whole again, never be able to pick up the pieces and build anything that isn't just a sorry imitation of what you had.

Yet you will. You will get better. You will forge a new normal, and it will have its beauties and wonders too. There may be some emptiness still, but I try to think of it as the emptiness of Jesus' tomb. That kind of emptiness has the light of the Holy Spirit behind it. The scars may remain but Jesus has scars too. There is comfort in such thoughts. A person who has suffered a loss needs comforting thoughts.

The loss of a child fills a parent with many emotions. I think all parents have imagined it, with their chests tightening at the very thought. The mother feels that sickening dread when the school bus comes by and her child is not on it. The father feels it when his child disappears in the park when he is fishing the stray ball out of the bushes. The parents who wait in the hospital corridor wondering if the operation was successful feel it. The lives of children are so fragile.

Yet in most cases, children come through their childhoods, adolescences, and young adulthoods all right, intact. The recuperating powers of children from falls, injuries, cuts, bruises, and even broken limbs are legendary. They learn to walk by falling down, over and over again! However, many don't make it—more than we realize sometimes. We all probably know someone who has lost a child, or we know someone who knows someone who has.

In our country, each year thousands of parents bury adolescents who have died in car accidents, sometimes with the element of impaired driving thrown in, whether it is drinking or alcohol, drugs, or simple cell phone texting that caused the impairment. Those thousands of parents go through all the guilt, blame, recriminations, and "if onlys" that the death of a child entails. You can't turn the calendar back and snatch back time, although you wish over and over again that you could.

There are the increasing numbers of American parents who bear the sorrow of having an adult child die of a drug overdose and all the additional stigma and shame that goes along with that. There are large numbers of parents whose promising, bright children die of leukemia or other diseases. These parents wonder why their beloved children were stricken while their neighbors' and friends' and relatives' children thrive.

Yes, thousands of Americans lose children every year, yet most of the time we believe that all these tragic things happen to other people far away, not to us, not up close and personal. We shudder and turn away from the heartrending newspaper photographs of a missing or murdered child, wondering how the parents bear the grief; if they will ever smile or be happy again, or if their dreams will be haunted till they die. Maybe we even have some unworthy thoughts: we think that when bad things happen to people, they must have lost God's favor somehow to have such tragedy befall them. Judging and being judged is so much a part of being a parent! We blame and praise parents for everything children do.

"Johnny up the street got into trouble, so his parents must not discipline him."

"Karla down the road got a full scholarship, so she must have good parents."

"Kevin across town died in a car accident—his parents must have not taught him how to be a careful driver."

"Patty just married a wonderful guy—she had the influence of her great parents!"

It is better to leave all such thinking up to God: His judgments are true and righteous altogether. Ours are limited and blind. We simply do not know the what and why of it all; why one child flourishes while another is taken. Part of our unworthy thoughts may be that maybe those parents who lost children didn't look after their children properly to keep them safe and healthy. After all, that is a parent's job, isn't it? Yet most parents who lose children were caught just as unawares as we might have been when tragedy struck. They didn't do anything differently than we might have done.

We may even think that God loves us too much to let such a thing happen to us, even as we cringe at our own arrogance and conceit, all the while knowing that these kinds of thoughts are rooted in fear: fear that this could very well happen to us, because it can happen to anyone. It does not only happen to non-believers or to the unlucky or the poor, to child abusers and neglecters or to that vast sea of "others" who are somehow different from us. It can happen to us, and at any moment. It happened to me and my family. After many heart-wrenching moments, I have come to trust God with this profound loss.

I can confirm that it is the worst pain ever. Yet I am not alone in this parental hurt. The Children's Defense Fund says that each and every day sixty-four babies die before they have reached their first birthday. At least twenty-two children or teens die in an accident each day; eight children or teens die by gunshot wound, and thirty-seven more children are wounded by the same. Seven children or teens take their own lives each day. The National Cancer Institute says that each year nearly two thousand children die of cancer: four or five per day.

Put into time frames, these statistics mean that a baby dies every twenty-two minutes—a baby who will never see his or her first birthday.

Every hour and six minutes a child or teen dies from an accident.

Every three hours and eight minutes, a child or teen dies of gunshot wounds.

Every three and a half hours, a child or teen commits suicide.

Every six hours, a child dies of cancer.

Behind those sad statistics are grieving parents—parents who wish they could turn back the hands of time and have a "do over." Even parents of cancer patients must wonder, "If I'd only noticed the symptoms sooner", or "If only we'd gone with the more expensive treatment." They think, "Maybe we shouldn't have tried the last operation" or "Maybe we should have tried one last operation."

The second guessing may go on for decades. Yet all the second guessing and "if onlys" in the world don't change anything. You can't take it back, whatever you think you might have done differently to have avoided your particular loss.

The lingering thoughts of "if only" fade in time, and you

realize that what is . . . simply is. You cannot undo what was done. You did about the same as anyone else would have done in your circumstances as you went about your day-to-day life and made your decisions. Others have made worse decisions, and they and their families were all right. You were doing your best with what you knew to do. Eventually, you come to accept what happened. What is gone is gone. Yet you never, ever forget.

We may never know why we had to suffer a particular loss. We may not know for a very, very long time and maybe not on this side of eternity. After a time you stop wracking your brain trying to figure out why. Then you just walk your path as best you can.

Since I have walked this path of a parent grieving the loss of a child, surely one of the greatest losses on the earth, I would like to ask you the reader to stay with me as I write about my path toward healing, peace, and even happiness after a devastating loss. I believe the lessons I learned apply to any kind of loss.

I always knew I must write this book to help people who are going through grief to cope with their difficulties. It is not an easy task, but I feel it is a mandate from God. I am writing to help people, not just those who have lost a child, but anybody who has lost something precious and important. The truth is, everyone will suffer from loss. After Jacob died, I read books about other people's stories, and it helped me a lot. I want to help others with my story too.

Maybe you lost your innocence, your marriage, your parent, or a job that fulfilled you and gave your life worth. Maybe your loss is that you have never found the thing you have been looking for, the thing you know will bring you happiness. Or maybe you achieved that thing yet still feel empty and are mourning the years lost pursuing an unsatisfying dream. Maybe your losses are financial, or you have suffered from a loss of reputation. You might have experienced the agony of infertility, where hope rises and then is dashed down again, sometimes time and time again. There are many kinds of losses. They all hurt.

Since I have gone through such a profound loss—a loss that no one could shrug off—I feel I am equipped to help people who are suffering. I have been in those deep, painful valleys. I have literally walked through the valley of the shadow of death. I made it out and so can you. I can testify that even in the face of the greatest loss, there can be consolation, comfort, and even happiness in the end. I can assure you that, even with the most profound loss, someday you will be able to love and even laugh again. You will be able to experience peace and joy, more and more as time goes by.

I pray you too will find peace and surcease from your pain; I pray you will find rest through the Holy Spirit, your Comforter. I hope you become more aware of the Holy Spirit that is inside you and commune with Him daily so He can console you.

Even if you aren't a believer, I wish this for you.

Faith in God is paramount to me and to my recovery from loss. It helped me to find meaning in my loss and to heal more quickly than I would have without it.

Faith also gives me the hope—no, the certainty—that I will meet my Jacob again.

This is my journey of faith. I've often said that the greatest leap of faith I ever took was to let Jacob go that day.

While I walk through the memories of dealing with the greatest grief of my life, I ask you to read slowly and to please listen as the Spirit speaks to you. Many times in this book I write what the prophetic voice speaks, and I believe it might a specific word for someone. Receive it, I pray, in Jesus' name.

God's will can only happen if we reject the enemy's plan to abort our purpose and vitality by taking away that which was precious to us. I want to share my story with those who are grieving and brokenhearted. I also want to assure the reader that, no matter how dark or cold it may be in this valley, there is sunlight. He will lead us and shed His warmth and sweet grace ahead.

Walk out of this valley with God. He is there, even in the valley of the shadow of death, because the Lord is your shepherd, and He will never leave you.

Psalm 23:

The LORD is my shepherd;
I shall not want.
He makes me to lie down in green pastures;
He leads me beside the still waters.
He restores my soul;
He leads me in the paths of righteousness
For His name's sake.
Yea, though I walk through the valley of the shadow of death,
I will fear no evil;
For You are with me;
Your rod and Your staff, they comfort me.
You prepare a table before me in the presence of my enemies;
You anoint my head with oil;
My cup runs over.
Surely goodness and mercy shall follow me
All the days of my life;
And I will dwell in the house of the LORD
Forever.

Chapter One

My Destiny

That terrible day I was asked a lot of questions that led up to an unfolding of tragic events.

It all happened so fast. If I had only known how the chips would fall, I would have done things very differently. It seems like everything just went all wrong. I should have said, "No, no, no," when opportunities came to do so. I wish I could erase the questions to which I said, "Yes, yes, yes," or I could erase my answers. Maybe then I could have changed the sad ending. Or maybe not. Who knew what would happen that day? God knew, and He does order my steps.

My own mother told them, when it happened, "Get Lynn! Get Lynn!" and they did. I wish they would have never have come to get me with that awful news. Then maybe—what? It wouldn't have happened? Could things have been changed? Of course, you go to get the mother when a child is injured. That's the only logical thing to do.

Yet I wish no one had ever come to me with those awful words, "There's been an accident . . . Jacob . . ."

By then events had lined up so that I was going to lose my baby.

What forks in the road that could have been taken to change things had already been passed by.

This is part of the agony of a loss. We always want to second guess and think, 'If only I had done this . . . or not done this . . . If only things had turned this way instead of that," et cetera. We try to adjust the dials of the past just a little bit to see if the result is different.

I still wish I could turn back time and change something here, tweak something there. Maybe then the end result would have been different.

Every night I awaken and remember, and I find myself praying that it was just a bad dream. Yet I have that sinking feeling in my stomach and I remember that it is real, and my child is dead and nothing will ever be the same after what happened that cold December day, two days after Christmas.

There was already a solemn atmosphere surrounding that winter day. My adopted aunt's eighteen-year-old grandson had died in an automobile accident before Christmas. Now it was two days after Christmas, on a Friday, and the funeral for her grandson was today.

The day before, Thursday, Jacob had stayed with his cousin, Shepherd, and his family. They were in town visiting from Atlanta. Every Thursday afternoon I had to go to Macon to pick up payroll, so Jacob played with his cousin Shepherd, who was his age.

I remember telling Shepherd's dad, Darren, that Jacob had been a little melancholy since Christmas. Looking back now, I don't think he had any kind of foreknowledge that he was about to leave us. Yet it was just a reminder that he had always been somewhat sensitive and emotional.

Throughout his life, Jacob had struggled with different little nervous habits, like picking at sores and his fingernails. The only real illness he had, though, was when he was only about one and a half years old. He'd had a rectal prolapse as a result of diarrhea. It was similar to hemorrhoids but much more serious. All this confused Jacob very much, and it affected him. He did get better, but he was so nervous about it happening again, he would let himself get very constipated in order to avoid a repeat of the incident. This was a problem until he was four years old.

I remember his first T-ball game at Twiggs Academy. His stomach was huge because he had been holding it in, and then the pangs hit him. We had to run around looking for a bathroom right before the game. It was so sad. Also, it happened one year when we went to the beach with my mom and dad. Jacob was very bloated and even doubled over in pain. It was pitiful. I bought some mineral oil to put in his drinks, which the pediatrician had told me to do. He hated it, but I told him he was going to have to take the medicine, so he ran off to the back bathroom. We didn't even realize he was gone. All of a sudden he came running into the kitchen, saying, "You've got to come look, everybody! It's Mount Everest!"

Sure enough, when we got to the commode, it was the biggest poop you ever saw a little boy do! It was a great victory! We still laugh about Mount Everest.

That was Jacob. Whether he was sick or well, he was the center of family concern, attention, and laughter.

On Thursday night, December 26, 2002, there had been a visitation for the young man who had died in the car accident. Jacob had stayed with his older brother Blake while I attended it, and he was so excited because while he was being babysat, he was going to go to a "party at the cabin".

The cabin belonged to my cousin David who was always telling Jacob to come to a party there. Many times I had refused this invitation because Jacob was too little. Jacob begged me a lot about going along with the older kids to the cabin. I usually didn't let him go, but I did let him go that Thursday night because it was a family party.

I attended the funeral visitation, and it was very sad. I don't remember much about it; I just remember feeling a very heavy spirit as I walked out of the funeral home. I began to speak in the Holy

Spirit under my breath. This continued as I got in my car and rode home.

Looking back, I sometimes wonder: Was there some prophecy involved in the heavy spirit I felt as I left the funeral home after the visitation for that young man? Was I getting messages about things that were to happen in my family the very next day? I think I was.

I'd had other spiritual experiences like it. The year Jacob was born, 1997, our family had two divorces—one on each side. All the people involved also went to the same church, which meant there were many layers of relationships and connections. It was complicated and awkward. There were six small children involved, all of whom had grown up with my children because they were their cousins on both sides. I spent lots of time helping with the children and trying to be as neutral as possible, but it was the saddest thing I ever witnessed for the children involved.

One day while interceding in my room through prayer, I was overwhelmed with grief regarding the six children, especially the only girl among them: Kassi, who was the same age as my daughter Leslie. They were very close. I was caught off guard by my anguish as I spoke in my heavenly language of prayer. I felt a very heavy spirit on that occasion also, like a spirit of death. I was grieving through my prayers, as it says in Romans 8:26-27: "Likewise the Spirit also helps in our weaknesses. For we do not know what we should pray for as we ought, but the Spirit Himself makes intercession for us with groanings which cannot be uttered. Now He who searches the hearts knows what the mind of the Spirit is, because He makes intercession for the saints according to the will of God." I was no doubt being prepared for my own tragic loss of Jacob. The Spirit was interceding for me and Kassi.

I dismissed it, though, and I wondered to myself why I was so upset about someone else's kids. Although I loved them, it seemed to me you should only feel that grieved if it's your own child being affected. Yet I was specifically praying for Kassi. Kassi was driving the ATV (All Terrain Vehicle) in the accident with Jacob. Bless her heart.

I've no doubt now that I was being prepared for the death of a child that would happen in the midst of what had been a very complicated situation, fraught with a lot of emotional connections on all sides. It was almost as if I was pre-grieving, anticipating the bad things that can happen in a fallen world, even during the Christmas season.

After all, even after our own personal "Christmas"—when we receive Jesus as our Savior—things do not always go well. Being a Christian or faithful believer does not mean that bad things will not befall. After the very first Christmas, many mothers were plunged into grief when Herod ordered the massacre of the innocents out of jealousy and the threat he felt to his power by the rumors of the newborn Christ child. Every Jewish child two years old and under was killed. Matthew 2:18 tells of how, after this genocide of babies and toddlers, and even the great ancestress of the Jewish people, Rachel, could be heard weeping along with the mothers for the children of the Israelites: "A voice was heard in Ramah, lamentation, weeping, and great mourning, Rachel weeping for her children, refusing to be comforted because they are no more."

I was to begin weeping with Rachel just two days after Christmas over the loss of my innocent child.

Blake and Leslie asked to spend the night at David's cabin after they'd all had a cook-out and "party" there. I said okay for them, but insisted that Jacob had to come home. I also stressed to Blake that he had to return home the next day by 8:30 a.m. to babysit Jacob so I could go to work. Blake agreed.

That night Jacob helped me take the ornaments off the Christmas tree. Then he was busy putting together some new Legos. There was a funny little story about those Legos. Jacob had seen the sets in the front of the store when we were running in for some last-minute items a few days before Christmas. He stopped and begged me for them, and I told him it was too close to Christmas. His reply was,

"But they will make me smart!" Such a cute little trickster! How could I deny a request like that? I sneaked out and bought them for him. He was so excited to see them on Christmas morning, I was glad I had bought them. He put them together that night and left them lined up on top of the couch—three little robot-looking things.

I was tired and ready to go to sleep. I told him to just come on to bed when he was finished putting them together. About thirty minutes later he came to get in the bed with me and his daddy since Blake and Leslie were gone.

Almost every night Jacob would promise to sleep in with Leslie if she'd read him books. She would read to him, but then, when she was done, he'd go over to Blake's room to sleep with him. He did this almost every night.

"Mama, that's not fair!" Leslie would say.

Then Blake would get involved. He would tell Leslie no, she couldn't have Jacob that night. He would sweep Jacob away to his room, and that was the end of that.

It was just sweet to me how much everybody loved him. He was the youngest in the family. Needless to say, he was spoiled!

When Jacob wanted to sleep with us that night because Blake was gone, I suggested that he sleep in his new sleeping bag on the floor beside our bed. He liked that idea and cuddled up there.

I got up early to fix cinnamon rolls for my aunt's family as an offering to help them in their sorrow over the loss of their nineteen-year-old grandson. While the rolls were baking, I sat down with my Bible, took my time, and had a good read while having my coffee. This was my favorite time of each day! I often wonder what I read that day, but I cannot recall. I trust it was just what my spirit needed for what would turn out to be the worst day of my life. Yet there was no hint of what was to come.

The rolls were ready, so I called my mama to see if my daddy could stop by and take them over to my aunt's home. Daddy was busy, so I called Blake. It was only about 7:45 a.m., so I was not sure if Blake would answer, but he did. I asked him to come over and take the rolls. He said okay.

Jacob walked into the kitchen right as I hung up the phone with Blake. I fixed his breakfast and put in a new movie he had gotten for Christmas: *Rescue Heroes*. Blake showed up in a few minutes to take the cinnamon rolls to my aunt.

Our homes, the cabin, and the family business were all within a few miles of one another, so getting around didn't take long. I told Blake to come right back home after he delivered the rolls because I wanted him to watch Jacob. He suggested that Jacob just go with him because he wanted to go back to David's. He said he could take Jacob there too after they delivered the rolls.

I said okay. This is one of the times when, looking back, I wish I had said no if that would have meant things turned out differently.

I went into the living room and asked Jacob if he wanted to go with Blake to deliver the rolls and then to Uncle David's. (We called him "Uncle" even though David was my cousin.) I told him he could take his movie with him if he wanted to.

He said, "Yeah," very excitedly.

I got Jacob's new Buzz Lightyear sweatshirt and jeans out, dressed him, and handed him his boots and his movie. I kissed him, and out the door he went.

It happened so fast. It was so ordinary. Yet it was the last time I would see my child alive.

Blake and Jacob took the cinnamon rolls to Aunt Peggy's. Blake brought them to the door while Jacob stayed in the truck. Aunt Peggy waved to Jacob. That was the last time she would see him alive too.

She told Blake, in regard to the car accident involving her grandson: "You just don't ever know when something like this is going to happen."

Blake said, "Yes, ma'am."

Since I had gone to the visitation the night before, I decided not to go to the funeral itself. Instead, I figured I would go ahead and get some of my work out of the way at the office.

When I got to the office, it was quiet. The other ladies were not there because Christmas was on a Wednesday that year, and they were not coming back till Monday. My mom was gone to the funeral. My dear friend Cathy, who worked with me there, has often said she was so glad she wasn't there that day. I understand. She was Jacob's Sunday school teacher, and he had hung out with us at the office a lot. He called her Aunt Cathy. She loved him and she would always give him treats at work. He told her that Grandaddy was not the boss, "God was," when she would tell him she had to work for Grandaddy because he was the boss.

I worked in my office all morning, doing payroll, paying landowners, and writing out bills. I was starting to feel excited about the weekend ahead. It was that TGIF (Thank God It's Friday!) feeling, where I had the satisfaction of having caught up on my work, leaving me clear-minded for a nice weekend.

Blake called me about 11:30 a.m. to ask if he could take the new tires he had gotten for Christmas to Jeffersonville. He wanted to have them put on by his uncle Keith there. Kevin and Kyle, his cousins and buddies, would go with him.

I said, "What about Jacob?"

He said, "He can stay here."

Again, I wish I had said no when Blake asked that. I forgot that they were at David's house. I thought they were back at our home because that had been the original plan. It slipped my mind that Blake had taken Jacob with him to David's.

I asked Blake who was there to watch Jacob, thinking "there" was our house.

Blake said, "Leslie, Kassi, and Kolby."

My mind was on the day before, because they were all at my house the day before. I pictured them at my house. I thought to myself that Jacob would be safer at home than on the road, driving with all those boys, so I said yes, it would be all right if Jacob stayed there.

This particular "if only" has bothered me for years. If only I had answered this question with a "No." If only I had asked him to bring Jacob to the office, where I was, maybe it wouldn't have happened. That would not have been unusual. We'd done that many times before. Jacob had played around the office while I worked.

Years after the accident, I screamed out loud the words: "I forgot!"

Those two words said it all: "I forgot." I simply forgot important details when I made the decision to let Jacob stay. I forgot he was at David's house.

It was a small, simple, human error anyone could have made. I forgot, and the events began to unfold fatefully.

In the next few minutes, David came home to get ready for the funeral. Somehow they went to the cabin. Leslie and Jacob were swinging on the porch swing. Jacob asked Uncle David where he was going? Leslie told Jacob that he was going to a funeral. "What is a funeral?" Jacob asked. Some of Leslies last moments with her brother were spent describing a funeral to him. Then Jacob jumped on the bunk beds and they watched Home Alone. Jacob took a ride with Kassi on the ATV. A few minutes later, Kassi returned without Jacob, frantically telling Leslie and Kolby Jacob was trapped under the machine. They ran to him.

I was at the copier when the news of the accident came. My back was toward the door, but I turned around when I heard a noise outside. A lady from my church, Mrs. Jim Tuck, walked in.

All she said was, "I need you to come with me."

I said, "Okay," thinking maybe she needed me at my aunt's house to help with the food for after the funeral. That was all right with me. I had caught up on my work, and I was prepared to go with her.

Yet just then my niece Kassi followed in on Mrs. Tuck's heels, in tears, saying something about an accident. I realized then, just like a little glimmer, that something bad had happened. I said, "What is it?"

The accountant of our firm, who was in the kitchen, came out when he heard the commotion. With a look of severity, the lady from my church told him he needed to come with her too.

Somehow the name "Jacob" penetrated my complacent fog. In between Kassi's sobs, the words came out that my son Jacob was hurt; he had been in an accident on the four-wheeler or some vehicle.

I'd already raised one son: Jacob's older brother, Blake. He'd had his share of broken arms and other mishaps, so I wasn't too alarmed. A mother of boys gets used to this kind of thing. I thought maybe Jacob had broken an arm or some such.

Yet deep in my spirit, a voice whispered, "This is it."

This is it.

I had been praying for the Lord to use me more in my life. I had vowed that whatever it took, I needed to find my mission and calling in Him.

There was an old song sung by the Heritage Singers called *Whatever It Takes.* I had sung that song and its lyrics as a prayer, not actually thinking anything severe would happen: "For whatever it takes to draw closer to You, Lord, that's what I'll be willing to do . . . Take the dearest things to me, if that's how it must be, to draw me closer to You . . . I'll trade sunshine for rain, comfort for pain, that's what I'll be willing to do . . . For whatever it takes for my will to break, that's what I'll be willing to do."

I had sung that song and I meant it as a prayer at the time. It looked like God was answering.

Of course, later on, when I faced the reality of having one of the "dearest things" in my life taken from me, of "trading sunshine for rain" and "comfort for pain," I changed my mind and wanted to take the prayer back.

But I couldn't. God's will may be hard. Sometimes when we pray for His will to be done, we have to steel ourselves for what follows.

Somehow that morning I sensed that whatever had happened or was about to happen was part of my spiritual destiny. This was it. There would be no turning back.

"He Didn't Make it"

In the car, I began to babble about how upset Jeff, my husband, would be if Jacob was hurt while using the little four-wheeler we had just gotten him for Christmas. I had said he was not to ride it yet because he was so new to it. If he did, he was supposed to be with Blake and wearing a helmet. The people around me said that the accident was on an ATV.

I was going to get my purse, but at this point, I just walked out behind those who had come to get me and got into the car. I think I was already going into shock. All of us got into the car, and all were eerily quiet except for a steady, low sobbing from Kassi, my niece. She was the one who had been driving the ATV when Jacob got hurt. I could not cry or react.

After a few minutes, I came out of my fog enough to dare to ask Mrs. Jerri, the lady from my church, whether Jacob was conscious. She shook her head no.

Okay. That was not good, but I did not dare ask the next question that popped into my mind.

I think the Holy Spirit was praying within me because I could hear words in my head, but a part of my brain seemed to have shut off. I felt an amazing peace come over me. I felt I was almost out of my body.

I had not lost touch with reality. I knew that what was happening was real.

Yet words like "Don't be afraid, I am with you," and "I have prepared you for this day," and "You are strong in Me" filled my mind.

Time stood still as I braced myself for what lay ahead as the car stopped. I think I knew that Jacob was gone, but you can only accept so much into your mind. I am sure by this time I was slipping into full blown shock. Everything I did after this was as if I was on automatic pilot. I was almost totally out of my body.

I don't know how I got out of the car. Now, looking back, I can imagine angels ministering to me, helping me to get out of the car. Somehow, my feet were steady. I had never been to the cabin myself and barely glanced at it. My focus was on getting to my son.

As I walked toward the scene of the accident, I recognized many church members who were already there. I remember a lot of cars. The cemetery where my aunt's grandson was being buried was right across the way, and they had all driven the short distance over from there. I knew it had to be bad for them to be gathered like that. I just followed Mrs. Jerri, my eyes on the ground. This was not going to be something minor. I did not make eye contact with anyone, but I could feel their pity and their prayers. I drew strength from their presences.

We had to walk up a hill to get to him. I don't remember much about the surroundings, but then I saw him lying on the ground. I went to him, squatted to my knees, and took his hand. It was warm; this would change soon. As, Jacob, my baby, lay on the red clay, I began to talk to him. I think I knew somehow that he was already gone, but I thought he could hear me either way. I began to tell him that Mama was here now and that if he was going to go with Jesus, it was alright. I reminded him that I had taught him all about Jesus, and he could put his trust in Him. As my darling five-year-old lay in the red clay, a blue bruise at his ear, and a little blood coming out of his ear and his mouth, I remember looking upward into the sky as if to imagine his spirit leaving his body and going to Heaven. I felt as if an angel was guiding him. I knew he was not scared at all. I held his hand a few more minutes, wishing I had something soft to put under his head. I was concerned that there was no pillow; just cold, red Georgia clay. A man gave him CPR, and I asked this man if Jacob was breathing. I already knew the answer to my question, but when this man, a friend I recognized from the volunteer fire department, raised his face and shook his head, it was confirmed. Of course, my heart longed for a miracle, but inside I knew Jacob was gone. His hand was already growing cold, but I thought maybe it was my hand that was cold. A parent never gives up hope. We were hopeful all the way to the hospital and even while we were there.

I let go of Jacob's hand and stood up. Then I realized my other son, Blake, was behind me. Blake was sixteen then, the same age I was when I became pregnant with him. In a way, we grew up together. He was my whole world, yet I had been really strict with him too.

Now I asked him to hold me since his daddy was not yet there. He put his arms around me, but I felt resistance within him. He felt very stiff and angry; it didn't feel comforting. I wasn't sure what to think. Maybe he thought I was being dramatic. Maybe I was. Yet he was my son and my other son was not breathing. I needed him, but I did not realize he needed me more.

I never really cried tears at this juncture; I just choked up a few times. Later I was told that Blake himself had been crying bitterly before I got there and had run off into the woods, blaming himself. He had said it was his fault for leaving Jacob alone. He would go through many of the "If onlys" himself and was in no position to comfort anyone. He needed comfort himself, even though none of it was his fault.

This was a terrible burden for a sixteen-year-old. He was too young to be my shield and protector, and I am sorry I made it about me. I had always called him my little man when he was a baby, but on this day, he should have been allowed to be a boy, overwhelmed with feelings, with me comforting him and telling him he wasn't to blame. I can only imagine how it must have felt to face something like this at such a young age. A tragedy like this has many casualties, not just the person who was taken away.

A few years later, in 2008, around the time he was struggling with his own faith, Blake wrote this poem about Jacob's death. My husband Jeff found it in an old phone he was using because he was having trouble with his.

It only takes something as small as a song
For me still to wonder why it all had to go so wrong
Sometimes I look up into the sky and wonder
why our dreams were shattered
Mad at God as if nothing else mattered
Then ask Him for His love, knowing He
blessed us with an angel from above
If only one more time I could touch your face
This anger in my heart would be replaced
Fighting to hold back the tear from my eye
Pain in my soul; you left without saying goodbye
This cannot be the end
Knowing I will see you again
My little friend.
Blake Payne

Blake never talked about Jacob much after the accident, but when he would let down the wall, it was like a break in a dam and he would cry like a baby. The first sermon he ever preached was on "Breaking down Walls."

After Jacob died, we did communion every year at my mama's on Christmas morning. Blake would break down and cry and go running out. It got a little better as the years went by, but the first year it actually stopped was the year he had met his future wife, Ashley. He was leaving after breakfast to go see her in Tennessee. We noticed it and were so happy for him. God was restoring his joy and healing his hurt heart.

Their baby girl, Anslee Blaire Payne, was born on Dec.13, 2011. On the Christmas morning that followed, Ashley recalls finding Blake just crying while lying in the bed with Anslee.

Startled, she asked, "What is it?

He replied, "I just wish Jacob could know her."

Blake is so precious. He is the best daddy. He loves that baby girl so much. We all do; she has been like an angel sent from Heaven for our family.

On that cold day in December 2002, the ambulance came to the scene of the accident. I tried to help them park and ran to show them where Jacob was. As soon as they got to him, I turned and walked away. It was too much. I had to look away and regroup. I hugged my sister-in-law and told her she'd have to have us another baby. I think I was trying hard to be fine, even though I wasn't.

The effects of shock are funny. I don't think you are aware of much, really. Also, the Holy Spirit just took me over. I was not shaking or anything.

I don't remember seeing them put Jacob in the ambulance. Maybe I was trying to be busy so I would not have to watch that. Then I approached an EMT and said that I was Jacob's mama. Could I ride with him? Although in my weakness I knew my mind had all it could take at this moment, I also knew I had no higher calling or privilege than to say, "I am Jacob's mama." I still feel that way and always will. It seemed natural that I should ride with him to the hospital. The EMT told me it would be better if I didn't. In fact, they would rather I didn't, he said.

I admit I was relieved, deep down, as I knew they would be working on him, pounding on him, doing CPR and saying things I was not ready to hear, at least not without his father being there with me. I did not want to hear words like, "no heartbeat." I just could not take that, even though I pretty much already knew that Jacob was gone.

My mother, Blake, Leslie, and I rode to the hospital with Jeff's good friend and cousin, Bob Powell, who is also a preacher. We went in his sister's minivan, and I remember that we all had wet, red clay on our shoes as we got into the car.

As soon as we got down the road a bit, I asked Blake and Leslie how they had ended up at the cabin this day. As I mentioned, our house, our business, and the cabin were all within a few miles of each other. It would not be unusual for the kids to be there, but I was so confused about what had happened and how it had happened, and I wanted a little clarity. Blake reminded me that they had been at David's, and it seemed David had either taken them to the cabin or else had followed them there on the ATV.

It was no small ATV; it was really big, especially for the year 2002. Not many people had that size of an ATV. Kids in the country drive young (sometimes before they get their licenses). It's a very usual thing. There are a lot of big, serviceable vehicles in the country for all the outdoor work, from tractors to trailers to trucks, and young people often are behind the wheel.

Still, I always had tried so hard to resist this and insisted on helmets and being careful. Yet here I was, confused and stripped of all my control, not even knowing why my child, Jacob, had been at the cabin instead of safe at home.

I was still asking questions, trying to piece things together when my mom said something like, "Lynn that does not matter now." I agreed, although I said I was just trying to figure out how they got down there. Needless to say, the details were painful and confusing, and they taxed my mind. My mother was right; all that mattered now was how we would get through this day.

I asked if anyone had told my husband, Jeff, yet. No one knew. As many people as were down there by the accident, someone must have called him, I thought.

I was wishing I had my phone, but I did not want to delay getting to the hospital. However, we were going by the office, so I asked Bob to stop so I could run in and get my purse and phone. As I was running back out after getting them and was climbing into the van, I mashed the button on the radio by accident, calling the last person I had talked to. It was my husband Jeff. Jeff said, "Hey." I could tell by his voice that he didn't know, but I asked him anyway if he knew about Jacob. He said, "No." As I clambered into the van, I told Jeff that Jacob had had an accident on the ATV at David's cabin and that it was pretty bad. He said, "Please don't tell me that."

I said, "I'm sorry. You know I wouldn't say such a thing if it were not true."

Jeff's cousin Bob started sobbing out loud as he listened to our conversation. When he turned I could see the heartbreak all over his face. I'll never forget how he looked. It's never easy to see a grown man cry. He was hurting for Jeff, his friend and cousin, and he loved Jacob too. Everybody went very quiet. Bob would be the one to preach at Jacob's funeral.

Jeff had been working back in the wood yard alone when I called, and when he came out, his crew had already heard about the accident. They told him, "You had better go," without saying much else. He drove himself to the hospital, alone in the car for a long time. Yet he was not really alone. Calls from friends and relatives kept him company. Jeff has a lot of good friends. I think he has the most friends of any guy I know. This is a testimony to the fun, tender, loyal, spirit-filled man he is.

Jeff had another friend with him too. Jesus was with him as he drove toward what he must have known was going to be bad news about his youngest son. He recalls singing to himself *The Anchor*

Holds by Ray Boltz and Lawrence Chewning as he drove. The song tells of how "The anchor holds, though the ship's been battered," and how "the anchor holds, though the sails are torn," and how the singer fell on his knees "as I face the raging seas, the anchor holds in spite of the storm." Jeff sang to himself as he drove toward our new and painful destiny: "It was in the night, through the storms of my life, oh, that's where God proved His love for me." I am sure Jesus gave him strength through this song and the love of friends, church fellows, and relatives. It was enough to sustain him through that drive.

When our little group was on Bullard Road, about half way to the hospital in Macon, my phone rang. Someone informed me that they were taking Jacob to a smaller hospital, in Dublin.

That seemed like another confirmation he was gone. If there was any hope, wouldn't they keep him at the larger hospital where there were more sophisticated equipment and more surgeons? Macon was known to have a much better trauma ER than Dublin. This could only mean one thing. They did not need the more sophisticated trauma center in Jacob's case. It was too late.

My worst nightmare was coming true. A family's dread—the tragic loss of one of its prized members—was really happening. Our most innocent, precious gift from God was being taken away from us. I was numb. I could not even cry. Why, my God, have You forsaken me? echoed in my mind.

Yet I never really prayed for Jacob to live. I knew this was God's will. Somehow, God let me know within seconds of hearing of the accident that this was His plan and that I should let Jacob go in peace.

Now that I had my phone, I made a few calls to friends who probably had not heard yet. Then we got pulled over by the police.

Bob's voice trembled as he told the officer what we were doing, and then the policeman just shook his head. I could see his sorrow for us. The police already knew about the accident. Bob said, "This is his mama." I just looked at the policeman, and he said, "Follow me." So the last few miles to the hospital we had a police escort. It was becoming more real and dire by the moment.

When we arrived at the hospital, many friends were there to support us. Somehow I walked in. I don't remember much about it. Hospital staff took us to a small, private waiting room. Although I wanted to know more about Jacob's situation, I was frightened to take the blow by myself. I told them not to tell us anything until my husband Jeff arrived. Jeff is my rock and my soul mate. This day, most of all, he was Jacob's daddy.

We'd been together since I was thirteen. We were about to go through hell together. Each one of us in our family faced hell, together and alone many times, but we know we will be all together in Heaven one day.

Jeff finally arrived after about an hour or so of us sitting there, and they brought him to the small waiting room. I was so glad and relieved when he got there.

I don't even remember how they told us. Leslie said it seemed like it took forever.

She was sitting in her daddy's lap, taking comfort from his presence. At thirteen, she was way too young to have to see such a day.

It was a perfectly normal day. Leslie later reflected on how your whole world can turn upside down and change in just a few minutes on a perfectly normal day. They had only ridden for about ten minutes when Kassi came running through the door of the cabin, calling out that Jacob was hurt; he was trapped under the ATV. Leslie said it was like her whole world collapsed around her when she and Kolby and Kassi ran outside and then she saw Jacob pinned under that heavy vehicle. Try though they might, the three of them could not get the ATV off of Jacob. Leslie started to run, with Kassi and Kolby running behind her.

They saw a trailer on a dirt road and ran up to it to beat on the door and cry out for help. There was no answer. Then they ran down the main road, for miles. Leslie wore holes in her socks with all the running. My heart breaks to think of this thirteen-year-old girl running desperately, searching for help, trying to save her brother's life.

She ran into Mr. and Mrs. Tuck, who were driving down the road headed to the graveside service. They took her to the house of the family who was burying their own grandson at that very moment. My mother was there helping prepare the food for the crowd that would come after the funeral.

How relieved Leslie must have been to be able to pour this out to a grown-up, someone who could help—her own grandmother. Leslie told her of the accident, and my mother had to make the call to 911. I'm so sorry she had to do that about her own grandson.

Leslie took Mr. Tuck to the scene of the accident while Kassi came with his wife to get me. This man lifted the ATV while our darling Leslie pulled her hurt brother out from underneath it. I thank God for Mr. and Mrs. Tuck being our angels that day, but I am sorry for what they went through to help us. One young person was already being buried that day.

And my poor Leslie! So young, having to take so much responsibility for a terrible accident with her dear little brother trapped underneath a heavy vehicle as huge as that ATV. She must have feared to move her brother, yet been desperate to pull him out from under the weight that was crushing him.

She was a very, very brave girl that day, doing her utmost to save her beloved brother. She had nightmares about it afterward, and she felt terribly guilty. I guess when death visits, there is always guilt. Yet Leslie was a heroine that day, and she behaved without a fault. I get tears in my eyes when I think of my brave young daughter and her heroic deeds on such a horrific day.

Once the vehicle was raised, and she got her injured brother out from under its threatening weight, Leslie lay down next to Jacob to hold and comfort him, thinking and hoping it was all just a dream, but life had suddenly become a waking nightmare.

Of course, as we sat there in the hospital, we all had hope that

Jacob would pull through somehow. Our hopes ended in that small, family waiting room.

I don't remember how the hospital staff told us or who told us. I just remember hearing, "He is gone." And then a lot of crying.

Leslie's dad confirmed it through a murmur into Leslie's ear: "He didn't make it, sweetheart."

Leslie's teacher gave me this essay my daughter wrote about the death of her little brother.

THE DAY I LOST MY BEST FRIEND

It was about lunch time … Kolby, Kassi, Jacob and I were at the cabin, babysitting Jacob. Kolby was playing Nintendo; I was making Jacob's lunch and he and Kassi were about to go ride the mule (ATV). The pizza was hot, so they were going to ride while it cooled off.

Up to this point, it was a perfectly normal day. Who would have ever known that your whole world could change within a couple of minutes?

Ten minutes passed after the ride began; then Kassi came running through the door saying Jacob was hurt and trapped under the mule. As I ran to find him, it was like my whole world just stopped! I found him, and then my whole world dropped.

I ran to get help and to call 911, with Kassi and Kolby running behind me. We finally got help from one of our church members who were at the house up the road preparing a meal for a family that had buried their nineteen-year-old grandson that day. We ran to Jacob and finally got him out from under the mule. I just lay with him, thinking, "It's just a dream," but it wasn't. It was a waking nightmare.

We went to the hospital and waited for what seemed like forever for the results. I was sitting in my dad's lap. Suddenly I realized that people were crying more than they were before, and I asked Dad if the test results had come in.

That's when I found out the worst news of my life and heard the most terrible words come out of my father's mouth: "He didn't make it, sweetheart."

Well, I miss him already but I know that he is in a better place now. I also know that I will someday see him again and I hope that you will also.

We will one day see our Angel Ranger.

Love you, Jacob.

Your sister, Leslie.

Leslie Payne

Chapter Three

The First Aftershocks

The hospital staff let us go back into the treatment area to see Jacob. I went straight to my little son and kissed him. Struck by how cold he was, I shed tears for the first time. "He's so cold, so cold," I cried out loud in a kind of protest. Others who have lost loved ones told me they too were shocked at how cold the body of their loved one felt.

Jacob was my youngest child, my third one. He had been a surprise—a true gift from God. On her eighth birthday, Leslie had wished for a new baby for our family. Blake was eleven already, and she wanted a little baby to play with. I believe she had a sister in mind, but her prayers and hopes were answered in God's way: with a little brother! (She was very happy with that too!)

When we had learned that I was pregnant with Jacob, we prayed for a full term baby. Both Leslie and Blake had been premature. We wanted a baby I could bring home and nurse, not one we would have to look at through glass, attached to a lot of tubes at the hospital. Of course, we would have taken any baby, preemie or not, but we hoped this experience would be delightful from the start. We sensed the baby was a boy, and we decided to name him Jacob.

Even though I was sick during the pregnancy and had some

premature labor, with enough meds and bed rest, Jacob came full term on September 8, 1997. He weighed a perfect seven pounds!

Jacob was everybody's baby. We all worked together to raise him. Everyone pitched in changing diapers and in all aspects of his care.

Needless to say, he was spoiled rotten. He was a mama's boy, which I attributed to my nursing him. Also, I was older now, and I was not as uptight about rules like I was with Blake and Leslie. I let Jacob play in the mud and pick out his own clothes, even if he wound up wearing a ragged Power Rangers outfit! He was very funny and talked with the biggest Southern drawl you've ever heard.

Now my bright, funny, sweet little baby lay cold and still as people filed in to stroke him and say last words to him. I just sat in a chair in the hospital and watched as many friends and family members came into that sterile room and showered love on Jacob. I watched them, one by one, come in and kiss him and cry and tell him sweet things. He just lay there with a sheet over his little body, which only hours before had been full of life.

A parent should not outlive a child. There is something unnatural about it. I thought about Eve; how she must have felt when she was faced with the death of her son, Abel. Even Moses deems it worthy of mention in the book of Genesis that Haran, Lot's father, died before his own father, Terah (Gen. 11:28). It is significant when a child dies before the parents. There is truly the sense of something being felled, cut down, long before the proper time.

King David saw the death of his child. David begged God not to let his child with Bathsheba die. He fasted and prayed and prostrated himself upon the earth (2 Samuel 12:16). Yet the child was taken.

There really aren't very many human situations that you can't find some resonance with in the Bible. It is truly the book that has it all. What a comfort are its ancient notes that sound of human sorrow and suffering over thousands of years. God doesn't pull any punches when it comes to suffering. He knew we would need such a book in our direst and darkest hours, to know that others have suffered similar things before us. There are few, if any, human situations and troubles that are not depicted on its pages. It is packed with emotional expressions of how people feel in such times and guidance as to how to call on God and make it through such trials.

After thirty minutes or so of sitting there in the hospital treatment area, I began to drum my feet on the concrete floor in a kind of protest of what was happening as family members and others came in and out. I felt anger and resentment as the reality of the events hit me and I watched this drama unfold. Jacob's siblings, aunts, uncles, grandparents and other relatives were all crying and kissing him and loving on him while I softly beat the floor over and over with my feet as I sat in that chair. Each beat pounded loudly in my mind. Yet for some reason, I was able to stop before I "lost it." I just turned off my inner turmoil, coping somehow. I guess I was in emotional shock.

Of course, I knew that nothing could ever turn back the hand of time, although I wanted to be able to do so more than anything; I wanted to go back into the morning and turn the dials and change the routes and channels so that this outcome would be different. Yet I could not snatch back the moments before Jacob was hurt in the ATV; I could not go back and do things over again. Time was marching on. It was unstoppable and unchangeable, as was the past.

I was filled with anger and regret. As many people do when things go horribly wrong in their lives, I blamed myself. My heart screamed at me: "You failed him.

You let him down. He looked to his parents to protect him from all harm, but for some reason today you could not."

I was even ready to blame God.

I thought that it must have been the sovereign Lord who let Jacob's guardian angel step aside that day. I knew He could have stopped it, but He did not. Why?

How many human souls have cried out that word when tragedy befalls them: "Why?" We so seldom get an answer in this world, no matter how many times we ask, "Why, Lord? Why?" It was a question I was to ask many times.

I sighed and thought of Job 3:25: "For the thing I greatly feared has come upon me, And what I dreaded has happened to me." What parents do not dread the thought of an accident involving their child? What parent does not shiver at the thought of untimely injury, illness, or death to a precious child?

I had pleaded for the blood of Jesus Christ to cover my children in protection. Now I had to trust God even in Jacob's death. It was the biggest leap of faith I have ever had to take, the leap from disillusionment and a broken dream to trusting God again. It took some time to get there, too.

I had to reassure myself again and again that Jacob's spirit was safe in Heaven and that he was all right. Now our duty was to put his precious body to rest.

Our friend who runs the local funeral home came for Jacob's body. A nurse came out and asked me if I wanted his clothes, and I said yes. My cousin Dawn, in one of many small and considerate services to me, took the bag of clothes for me and offered to wash them. Jacob's poor little Buzz Lightyear sweatshirt was cut right through the thick logo over the chest.

We walked outside without our Jacob, on a December day that was strangely sunny. This just could not be happening. But it was.

It was just Jeff and me on the ride home. I don't remember us talking much.

He did echo my earlier thoughts when he said, "I feel like we let him down."

I also remember someone called Jeff's cell phone about something unrelated. It was hard to hear Jeff tell the man he had just lost his son. It was such a surreal feeling.

When we got home people were already there at the house. Jeff stayed in the yard with a friend to cut some firewood for the fireplace. I walked into the house alone. A few girlfriends of mine were there. I honestly don't even remember greeting them.

A special friend, Rhonda Nobles, who had been battling cancer for years was there, and she explained that she had taken out the

Christmas tree and had done all the other things on a list of things to do that I had left for Blake and Leslie. She also had taken Jacob's sleeping bag and a few other toys and Legos and put them in his room. She wondered if that was okay. I assured her that it was fine and that it was what I would have done.

Soon the house was full of many people. It was very moving. Even some friends from high school showed up. There were also some people whom I barely knew, but I was touched by the outpouring of genuine concern. The upstairs was full of Blake and Leslie's friends and cousins. The young people rallied around them at this time, and many of them stayed for the next few nights to be close and comfort my children, themselves, and one another. We have a large family and a wonderful church family too. How touching it was that they were there for us in the midst of our sorrow. Our family and our church family were vital to our bearing this loss. How beautiful is the body of Christ.

These memories still move me to tears. I cannot recall all the tender and meaningful gestures people made to support and comfort us. I assure everyone, though, that each one was noticed by us at the time. Not one went unnoticed by us or by Jesus.

I recall sitting on the couch with lots of people around. I kept saying I could not believe this had happened. At some point I started going through a drawer in the kitchen, looking for pictures of Jacob. Jeff and I had been separated in the crowd of people, but he happened to walk in the kitchen as I was pawing frantically through a drawer.

He said, "What are you doing?"

I just answered, "Looking for something," and described the picture of Jacob I was looking for. I was getting upset, and he knew it. He just looked at me with his gentle eyes and placed his hand on mine until I stopped what I was doing. Then I took a deep breath and leaned into him.

Soon I slipped away to my room, not sure what to do next. Upon entering my large bathroom, I locked the door. I mashed the "Play" button to hear the Jerusalem music tape my mentor, Pat Floyd, had just given me. I began to dance before the Lord with abandon. I had always done this sort of praise. Yet today this act of worship was deeper than ever before. Only the Holy Spirit and I together could face this sad day.

I played "Breath of Heaven" by Amy Grant to give me strength. I felt as if Heaven was where my heart was, and the breath of Heaven was all that could hold me together in the broken place. It was working; each thought and feeling I had to face, God helped me.

It was almost midnight when everyone left, including my brother and his wife, who had driven from Tennessee as soon as they heard. They had just returned to Tennessee from Christmas in Georgia! When they went to leave our house, they could not find their keys. Someone had picked them up by accident. They finally had to just leave their car and luggage.

You would think once we were alone that all Jeff and I would have done was cry. Somehow I was too exhausted, or else I was still in shock and denial. I know everyone reacts differently. I sensed too that a foundation had been laid. We were strong and somehow prepared for this, and we were facing it together. That counted for a lot.

Jeff and I got in our bed and turned out the light. Neither of us said a word. I do not remember thinking a single thought. We just silently embraced one another and clung to one another, like when David comforted Bathsheba after the death of their child (2 Samuel 12:24). We comforted each other physically and made love.

Then we fell sound asleep. I can't imagine how I slept, but I slumbered soundly until I woke up about four o' clock a.m., when my brain sent me a horrible message: "My child is dead. It really happened." Sleep had protected me a little from the pain, but the pain was inside me, poking me awake so that I could face it.

I rolled over on my side and began to weep. I cannot describe the depths of regret I felt. Death is so final. I knew nothing could make it not be so. This was my new reality. Whimpering, I begged God to let it be a bad dream, but I knew it was real.

Jeff woke right up, held me, and within seconds we were crying very loudly together, weeping and wailing over the loss of our son. I sobbed out that I was sorry I had woken Jeff up, and he said no, it was okay.

We had so much to face that day after Jacob's sudden death. It was the first day of a new and pained life without one of our children. We had to plan a funeral, see guests, and say goodbye. In a way, I now realize that all the things you do for someone right after they die are blessings. I had a few more moments with Jacob to look forward to, a few more things to do for my son.

So many years later the memory of those moments is still raw. As I write this my spirit cries, "My God, my God, why have you forsaken me" Of course, I know He has not forsaken me. It is just a desperate cry from a pained heart. As Jesus did, I don't say it to hurt Him; I just say it as an outcry so He can help me, so He can come nearer and know I need Him in that moment. Yet I am here to testify that He has helped me; He has never left me nor forsaken me. There is hope in Jesus.

I know the Lord must have wanted to turn His head away from our pain; the pain of losing a child; the pain He knows so well. Its depths simply cannot be imagined. He gave His only son up for us all, so God too has dealt with the untimely and violent death of a beloved child. In fact, if we are all God's children, God has had to watch many deaths of His children, some painful and unredeemed. He is indeed the king of suffering.

If you are grieving a loss, God will help you every step of the way, I promise, just as He helped me. He knows what you are going through. He has been there too.

Many days I spent sighing, as if merely to breathe was the hardest thing I had ever done. There is a reason they call it "grief stricken". Loss feels like a body blow so intense you are not sure you will recover from it. You have been struck; stricken. It hurts. Suddenly your life is behind a smothering wall of suffering, and you don't know if you will ever exist in the sunshine and fresh air of happiness again.

Yet you will. I pray you will. Survival of your child or anyone you love is hard work. Grief is a process you must take one day at a time, but life will come again if you walk with God and with those you love, and if you do not give up.

If you are facing loss, you are the reason I am writing this book. I pray you will live and not die from the terrible blow of your loss. I pray that the Holy Spirit will breathe on you His promise of new life and that you will believe in and look forward to the time promised in the Bible when all tears are dried and all things are made new again. As it says in Revelation 21, there will be a new Heaven and a new earth and even a new Jerusalem: "And God will wipe away every tear from their eyes; there shall be no more death, nor sorrow, nor crying. There shall be no more pain, for the former things have passed away" (Rev. 21:4). Those verses are the very climax of the Bible. What a glorious day it will be.

You will be able to dream again. God will pick up the broken pieces of your heart—the shattered dreams you have wept over so. He will say to you, one day, when you are ready to hope once more: "My child, it is time to dream again."

Dream Again

I never imagined much
I have just been a dreamer
Dreams came true one by one
I was just going along, dream after dream coming true
Until a nightmare became an intruder in my dreams
Standing there in my dreams, taking over my life
He was the thief in the night
My enemy swept over me like a flood

A lion seeking to devour me
He took my heart's desire
He chewed me and spit me out.

Now I imagine
Memories haunt me....
Imagine Peace
Dreams are forgotten
Grief waves cover me
I am floating "lifeless"
Imagining: "What are you going to do?"
Yet You allowed this
Your spirit You breathe into me
You are the river flowing through me
Your spirit is in me
You raise a standard against the intruder
And I am breathing again,
living again,
dreaming again.

Lynn Payne

Chapter Four

The Morning After

The morning after Jacob's death, Jeff and I walked to the kitchen when it was still dark outside. I still could not believe this was really happening. Jeff began to make us some coffee. I just looked around. My home had become unrecognizable with paper funeral home cups spread around, a commercial coffeepot, food all over, and in the doorway a stand with a guest book for signing.

This was our dream house, our home. In it, I had many collections. There were collections of antiques handed down from my family. There were scrapbooks about my kids, with all the information about them gathered in one place. I had a collection of journals too. I wondered if I would ever collect anything with such joy again. I feared all I would be collecting from now on were sighs, sleepless nights, and the pieces of broken dreams.

Like every mother, I had dreams for my children. Those dreams were always glorious and happy. There are no boundaries to what we parents hope our children will experience and accomplish; we wish every happiness and success upon them. We wish for them wonderful careers, loving and faithful spouses, beautiful children of their own who are full of accomplishments and good character, as well as heavenly, fruitful lives full of charity toward others. We dream that they will enjoy fulfilling and wonderful closeness with us, their parents, here on earth. Although more than anyone, we parents are aware of our children's weaknesses, we still see limitless potential in them that we hope will be realized; just as the Lord sees our limitless potential and encourages us in spite of our weaknesses.

Now those dreams for my family were shattered. Even my other children, Blake and Leslie, would be scarred by this, the loss of their little brother.

That morning Jeff and I had Krispy Kreme doughnuts—my favorite. It was better than the barbecue sandwich I had tried to eat the night before, but my desire was still dull. As we sat at our little table, Jeff said, "We had it all."

I just said yes and shook my head as if to mark the moment I realized our family would never again "have it all." In this moment of shock, I could only imagine a future as full of pain as the previous few hours had been. I am now thankful that I really did not have a clue how much warfare against sorrow and despair lay ahead of us; how much our family would be hammered by stress and strife when having it all had become only a distant memory.

There are times when after such a loss, you feel you will never be happy again. Your portion of happiness in this life seems like it had a large, permanent amount subtracted from it; that you will be forevermore operating at a deficit and that nothing can fill the void.

Everything in your life seems to be a mockery or to be meaningless, even the most treasured possessions you have. What does it all mean if the most precious part of your being—your child—has been torn from you?

"It's just stuff," I would say all the time. The things I once loved and collected meant nothing anymore without my Jacob. I was bitter, but God would not let me stay in bitterness.

Later, I was able to write this poem about it all:

> ## Collections
>
> I look around my house, my dream house
> Among my many collections, I look.
> Antiques handed down from my family
> Scrapbooks of my kids, my journals, my jewels
> The only thing I collect anymore are days of sighing
> Restless nights, broken dreams, broken me
> Can I ever be whole again?
> Can I ever be healed of my brokenness?
> The Holy Spirit says "Yes, the Healer is here
> Scars may remain, but I have scars too
> You are made in My image."
>
> **Lynn Payne**

I was always a take-charge kind of mom and handled most of the small stuff myself, but today I needed Jeff so badly. I couldn't have handled the details without Jacob's other parent there, someone who had loved him as much as I did and who was my life partner and friend.

Mother and father, husband and wife, we went upstairs to Jacob's room to get some clothes for him to wear in his casket. I knew I wanted Jacob to wear his navy sports coat, tie, and khakis. I worried that Jeff would suggest something more fun, like Jacob's football jersey, but we agreed to use it along with other special mementos to place inside of his casket, among other prized possessions and toys. I felt stronger just having Jeff with me, and I thanked God we were doing this together. Jesus, true love, family, and genuine relationships—these are the silver linings of the most terrible times of our lives.

Blake and Leslie both had cousins and friends spend the night. The teenagers were everywhere, lying on the floor and in the beds, and we were careful not to wake them. These kids were devastated. Jacob was everybody's little buddy. He wasn't like most five-year-olds. He thought he was as big as they were. His vocabulary showed it when he used slang words in imitation of the older kids. He did not understand why he couldn't watch *Spider Man 2*, which was rated PG-13. He would always ask what the "rate of" a movie was. *Spider Man 2* was one he really wanted to watch with Blake. Every day he would beg, "Please? Please?" Finally one day we made a deal.

He asked, "When I am thirteen, can I please, please watch it?"

"Sure," I replied, laughing to myself. By the time Jacob was thirteen, that movie would be so out of date. I knew he wouldn't be interested in it anyway. Little did I know he was not going to watch it at age thirteen—that or any other movie. By the time my little Jacob's thirteenth birthday came, he had been gone from this earth for eight long years.

One of the first people to visit us that first morning was a friend we went to church with, Don Sanders. His son has muscular dystrophy. He usually kept to himself, but I believe the Lord impressed upon him to come over. Just seeing Jeff and him sitting at our small kitchen table released an unspoken strength in me. I felt very heartened by his visit; this man who had "lost" the healthy, normal child we all dream about. His wife and I have become close friends. Their testimony is not so much in words, but in the life they lead every day as they take care of their dear son, Matt.

Later that morning we met with the funeral director about the times for the visitation and service and to decide who would preach at the ceremony. We asked our pastor, Gary Walker, and Jeff's cousin, Bob Powell, to do the service. Jacob's children's church pastor, Jeff Johnson (or "Butterbean," as Jacob had named him) was our choice to speak at the graveside. We had to choose pallbearers too. We chose Jacob's uncles—my three brothers and Jeff's three brothers.

These are the kinds of duties you never, never imagine you will have to do for your own child, and doing them is like walking through a bad dream. Yet you do what you have to do. Just when you are dealing with the shock of a death, you have to plan the funeral. It all happens so quickly. I think it is God's mercy again. In the first numbness and shock of grief, you are very busy. You don't have a lot of time to think. You must think, plan, and make decisions as to how to say a fitting goodbye to your precious loved one.

We had to order a small casket. Yes, they do make them for those especially tragic times when a child has died. They asked what we would like, and I just said something that looks like a little boy, maybe something wooden.

We asked Jeff's brother Terry and our sister-in-law, Rebecca, to do the flowers. They agreed as they broke down in tears at this request. Next, we talked with our friend and music minister, Brother Frank Hendrix, about the music. He had been Blake and Leslie's children's church pastor, and he is very sensitive and creative.

As we sat in my office, he asked me about any special memories I had. I recalled having awakened a few nights before Christmas to an icy blue light shining from the outside. I thought it was snowing. I had walked outside, thinking Jacob would be so excited about snow coming, but it was just a heavy frost. However, I had never seen such beautiful stars, and I just worshiped and thought of Mary and all she went through on her journey to Bethlehem.

As I explained it to Frank, I realized that it had been a special time God had given me to prepare me for what I would face. His message was that Jacob was like a star shining down on us. Thus, we decided Frank would sing "Twinkle, Twinkle, Little Star." The story got around, and a star became a symbol of our Jacob. It was actually good to have something to plan to honor him. These were the last things I would be able to do for my son.

Everything happens for a reason, and God's mercy is evident

everywhere, even in the death of a loved one. You really have to look for it, but you will find evidence of His love.

I think the way we see our children is how God our Father sees us. He loves us with the same unlimited dreams of our potential. He made us just how He wanted us, and that is what makes each one of us a masterpiece. Surely, too, He sees many of His dreams for us shattered as we make our mistakes and as life takes its punches at us and goes about its many unexpected twists and turns. How we respond is really what makes or breaks us as far as fulfilling our full potential. Yet a child is nothing but potential! From the moment you first look at your child, you are overcome with love and pride in this little masterpiece and all his or her possibilities.

Children are truly a gift from God, and I treated Jacob as such. When Jacob was little I was very focused on spiritual things. I taught him about Jesus and Bible stories, and also about the armor of God, which he could name. His fifth and last birthday party was a swimming party at his grandparents' pool and with the theme "Bibleman". I was trying really hard to bring him up properly in the Lord, but anyone who knew him knew he was pretty obsessed with the Power Rangers!

Yet one day when he was very small, I was reading my Bible and he sat beside me.

I said to him, "Go get one of your books to read beside me."

To my surprise, he brought his little Bible and pretended to read.

This became our routine. I would tell him he was going grow up to be my preacher, and he would just shake his head and agree. I will always cherish these moments in my heart and ponder over them.

Our dreams for our children do not always manifest in the ways we imagine. Yet God is always good. This precious little boy touched so many lives, and his life is preaching the most important message of all: Love Jesus and believe in Him because Heaven could be only a moment away.

Chapter Five

Love in the Midst of Pain

One of the hardest things was going to the cemetery to choose a plot. As we neared the turn toward the graveyard, I began to cry out loud. It was one of the first times I cried in front of people, and I was scared that I would lose control and just sob and sob forever, tears running down my face, unable to stop. I was, however, able to control myself before we got out of the car.

It was windy and cold as I got out of our new Ford Expedition. Jeff and my brother-in-law and a few more family members looked around and talked with the proprietor about details. They told him they wanted an area large enough for the whole family to be buried in over time. How ironic it was that the youngest in our nuclear family and the next to youngest in our whole clan needed the first plot.

Everyone insisted they wanted my opinion, but as the cold wind hit my face I cried out that I didn't care. I just wanted to run to the car, but somehow I stayed long enough and calmed down enough to agree on a spot.

All I could think about was how I was going to put my baby out there in the cold ground. The bitterly cold wind seemed to strip my breath away as well as strafe my heart.

From the beginning of humankind until the Lord returns, this ritual and necessity of burying the dead will always seem inhumane. Yet I also realize it is a blessing. Some do not get the chance to do this for their loved ones.

The Lord said, "Dust thou art to dust thou shalt return." It sounds very fine in the Bible, and it is easier when it is an older person, but I could hardly imagine it applying to my precious little Jacob whom I loved so. To me, he was the most beautiful little boy in the world.

I knew his spirit lived on, but his young body was precious to me too. I had washed him when he was dirty, dressed him in the best clothes I could find, held him when he was tired, comforted him when he was confused or scared, cared for him when he was sick, and dreamed of what he would look like when he grew up. I longed to hold his warm, living little body, in love and laughter, breathing again. Even though I knew his body was just the beautiful shell of his spirit, I still wanted to embrace him again.

Jacob had been the life's blood of our future and our joy. Now it seemed as if our future had flat lined. Medically, a flat line means the person is close to brain death or heart death. Yet people are often brought back from a flat line situation through resuscitation. Flat lining is like a pause between life and death when you are neither dead nor alive.

As a family, we were flat lining, stuck between life and death, veering toward death because of our tragic and terrible loss. Yet this kind of spiritual, mental, and emotional flat lining is just when God can resuscitate. This is when God reaches down and brings a person back to life, pulling him or her back from the edge.

God did bring life back to my family. He never chooses to let us remain hovering between life and death, though sometimes the rescue may take time, even years. He says no to our spiritual death.

He reached down, lifted up our family, and brought us back to life. Sorrow and grief can advance us toward the kingdom of God if in the midst of our trials we can praise God. Our trial and the many more to come were to humble us and to give birth to a miracle. I'm convinced that all trials serve that purpose.

If you are facing a moment of life or death, literal or spiritual, turn to Jesus. Cast your burden unto Him, for in Jesus' own words, He says, "Come to Me, all you who labor and are heavy laden, and I will give you rest. Take My yoke upon you and learn from Me, for I am gentle and lowly in heart, and you will find rest for your souls. For My yoke is easy and My burden is light" (Matthew 11:28-30).

That afternoon, after the visit to the graveyard to choose a plot, we went to the funeral home to view Jacob privately. The Holy Spirit was so close to us.

We noticed right away that his hair was not right; that was not the way he wore it in life. No doubt they had washed it to remove the blood, but they had blow-dried it out straight. I sent someone to go get some hair mousse from my friend's nearby beauty shop so I could style it the way Jacob always looked.

We admired the beautiful flowers my brother and sister-in-law had procured and arranged. I put Jacob's toys, bb gun, football jersey, and Power Rangers things in the coffin while we waited for the hair mousse. We all took turns kissing him.

When the mousse came, I fixed his hair. I think this was a blessing in disguise because I was able to focus on arranging Jacob's hair and not on the fact that he was in a casket. Friends and family just watched and all were excited and happy when I got done, saying, "Now that looks like Jacob!"

He was so beautiful. We resumed kissing him, crying over him, loving on him, and holding his little hands. He was cold. That was hard to bear. Yet if you think you can't touch a dead person, believe me, you can if it is someone you love. If it is your darling lying there, you will kiss the person again and again. I learned if I kissed him on his forehead, it did not feel as cold as the rest of his face.

When we arrived home I walked straight to my room. I had to be alone with God to worship Him.

A few minutes later Jeff knocked on the bathroom door and said, "I know what you are doing in there."

I opened the door, and he stuck his head in and gave me a kiss as if to say, "Carry on," and went back to our guests.

Jeff has always seemed to understand my love relationship with the Lord. He encourages it and seems proud that I try to be a woman of God. He, on the other hand, does not have to try as hard. His nature is very transparent; he seems to reflect God so naturally. Even at 200 plus pounds, Jeff is very gentle. There is no doubt in my mind that Jeff is a mighty man of God. He never so much as raised his voice to me in the years after Jacob died. He did everything he could to help me. I tried to help him in his grief too, as men are not as open about showing their emotions as women.

Sometimes it is hard to believe that anyone suffers more than the mother in situations like these. After all, this is the baby she carried in her womb for nine wonderful, expectant months. This is the baby she gave birth to in pain and joy. This is the infant she nestled at her breast and gave of her own nutrition to nurture. This is the child she held and helped to walk and whom she dressed and fed and tucked into bed. A mother's relationship with her child is so intimate, so deep. It is hard to think that anyone can grieve for a lost child like a mother does.

Yet sometimes I would realize when Jeff was in the shower that he was weeping in there. Jacob used to take showers with him, and he would stand on the built-in stool and swing on the towel bar, and the laughter would fill the house. I knew because of this that the shower was Jeff's safe and sentimental place to cry. Although I was pretty consumed with my own grief, it would hit me what was going on in there when Jeff took a long time in the shower.

I'd just walk over and say, "I know what you are doing in there." I would pull back the curtain and kiss him.

I realize we are the exception and that statistics say most couples don't stay together after such a loss. I am not judging anybody because I can surely understand. The stress levels around my house were enormous for probably the next ten years.

All I can say is, it was only by the grace of God that we held it together. It can be done. Try not to give up on each other or your family. Still try to have fun together and do romantic things for each other, no matter what losses or sorrows you are walking through.

I always kept it in mind that Jeff is Jacob's daddy, and I know Jacob would want nothing more than for us to take care of each other and to nurture his brother and sister. I like to think we followed the examples given in the Bible and turned to each other in hard times. That is really what marriage is all about.

Ecclesiastes 4: 9-12 says: "Two are better than one, because they have a good reward for their labor. For if they fall, one will lift up his companion. But woe to him who is alone when he falls, for he has no one to help him up. Again, if two lie down together, they will keep warm; But how can one be warm alone?" In the cold, dark, long nights of the soul that follow a death or any kind of tragedy in life, it is good to have someone to cuddle with in marriage. A dear friend once told me I was the most romantic person she knew. I took it as a compliment. I believe we all love a good love story. My passion (my love story) is so beautiful to me. Jeff is my soul mate. We met when I was just twelve and he was sixteen.

I remember that day I first met Jeff like it was yesterday. For some reason, I had to ride home on the varsity bus after my away game of junior varsity basketball. My older cousin Darren and Jeff got on the bus too.

Darren spotted me and said, "This is my spastic cousin, Lynn. You two ought to get along good since you are crazy too, Jeff."

We shook hands politely, but Darren was right. We had instant chemistry and soon we were just cutting up. When the bus made a stop, Jeff got up and came and sat with me. Smooth move! Then the bus broke down, and all the students had to stay at a motel overnight. What an adventure.

I wondered if Jeff and I would talk some more the next day.

Jeff seemed so refined and grown-up in his corduroy sports coat; he even ordered a coffee at Hardee's the next morning! It was pure excitement to see him and yes, he did sit by me again. Lord knows it was not because of my looks. We still laugh about how my broken glasses were held together with freezer tape, but he recalls thinking I was cool and had potential!

The bus broke down again on the way home, giving us a few more hours together. We both agree that our souls had mated by the time we got off that bus.

The following Monday Jeff managed to find me during class changes, even though his classes were down the hall from mine. After that, we hung out at school every day. A few months later he gave me twenty dollars on my thirteenth birthday, along with a sweet card. We had kissed for the first time a few days earlier, and it was official—the deal was sealed!

Although we could not really date, we managed however we could to spend time together. Jeff came to church to see me, and I would see him at my cousin's. The next year I cheered for varsity, and we were together at practice every afternoon and had many more bus trips together. Daddy would let him come over for visits, and we went to his senior prom on a double date with my brother and his girlfriend.

Young love can be very intoxicating. Our love story is one of make-ups and break-ups, mostly because of the age difference. I would burn out with the pressure of such an intense relationship. I was young and just wanted to be free. I needed time to realize he was the only person for me, whereas Jeff had always been clear about his love for me, staying close by, making it hard for me to forget him.

He was not perfect and broke my heart a few times, as I'm sure I did his, but I always knew he loved me. The last time we got back together he was a junior in college and I was a sophomore in high school. We had almost lost each other, and we both knew it, but I know God helped us. Our hearts were meant to be together, and although our passion would get the best of us, our love would see us through.

I was almost seventeen when I found out I was expecting. We were young and in love. With our parents' help, we were wed in a beautiful ceremony at my home.

Chapter Six

Family Life

Like most teens, I was distracted by my own agenda of fun and falling in love. Fortunately in my case, my husband is a wonderful man. We easily transitioned into grown-up life. Jeff quit college and began to work for my dad. I was very sick with the pregnancy, but other than that, I loved being a housewife and a soon-to-be mother. Blake, my firstborn, was precious to me, and I threw my whole life into his.

When Blake was about two, I started working with the preschoolers on Wednesday nights at our church. This led into helping also with children's church, the nursery, and later, the girls' clubs. I was not a natural teacher, but I tried. As a matter of fact, although it was my life's dream, even being a wife and mother were somewhat challenging. My nerves, hormones, and odd weaknesses were forever present. Even though I would put out a great effort, I struggled. I began to appreciate 2 Corinthians 12:9: "My grace is sufficient for you, for My strength is made perfect in weakness."

I had my second child, my daughter Leslie, in 1989. While I was pregnant with her, I was so sick I had to be hospitalized. I was so excited to have a girl! She was born two months premature and remained in the hospital a month. This was a very hard time. The

Lord began to teach me to press on even when I was weary and to continue to find strength in Him.

As things became more routine, I really desired to be used by the Lord, but I was so busy with my family that it was hard. I worked in my church whenever possible. Dreams of working in the mission field and saving the world seemed to be out of reach, but I heard the Lord whisper to me: "Your children are your mission field."

I tried to study the Bible. It seemed so hard to understand. One day while reading about Solomon, I felt the Lord really impress on me to also ask for wisdom. I understood this was not so that I could gain personally, even though I had always felt insecure about matters of the mind. I never felt smart in school and did not feel confident about working outside the home. That really did not matter to me, though. I was very fulfilled as a mother and wife. I desired this gift concerning Him and His world; to have the profound wisdom that comes from knowing Him and striving to be more like Him.

In 1997 I became pregnant with my third child. I had not really planned it, although I always knew I would have one more baby. I was older, and I really wanted to have a good pregnancy and carry this baby full term. I enjoyed it so much, and even though I was sick, it wasn't as bad as earlier pregnancies. I began to dilate early, but with meds and bed rest, I carried Jacob full term. On September 8, Jacob Karl Payne was born. I was able to nurse him, which was a first for me.

It was a wonderful time for us all. My son Blake, eleven years old by then and daughter Leslie at eight years old were so excited to have a baby brother! Jeff was really there for me, and he was really into this baby thing!

I liked it when he would say things like, "Be sure you clean his nose out with that syringe bubble thing, like the nurse said."

I would think, "Duh. This is my third child. I think I know." But I was touched by his enthusiasm and concern.

Jacob was our whole family's baby. We all pitched in to raise him, with the kids changing his diapers and all!

We had built our dream home and moved into it when I was about four months pregnant. It was hard to make ends meet without me working, so I cleaned the church and a few houses to take in a little extra money.

It seemed like this would be a great time of our lives. In general, everything became quite hard at this time. I was really being stretched with Blake playing in varsity sports and Leslie began to struggle in her school work at about this time too. We lived thirty minutes from their school, and I had to make several trips back and forth for many days because of their needs and activities.

I became exhausted. We took Leslie for psychological evaluation and ADD testing. Any parent who has been through this understands that it is very stressful. You feel like you are on trial and if there are problems, it's somehow your fault as a parent. She did get diagnosed with ADD, but because of her adequate progress in school (in consultation with her pediatrician) we decided not to medicate. She was insecure because of her schoolwork, and she also had some issues with being the middle child and having a new brother, a new home, et cetera. There were a lot of adjustments for her to make in her life. We had her tutored by Mrs. Linda Walker (our pastor's wife) and tried to help her as much as we could. I could relate to her difficulties in school. I think I had the same issues myself with ADD, and it was hard!

In addition to everything being very challenging at this time in my life, I did not feel like Jeff was sensitive to my needs and was not "getting it" that I was feeling very overwhelmed and somewhat depressed. I did not feel he was "there" for me as he had been when Jacob was first born. I had always had a short temper with the kids, but it seemed like I ranted and raved at them most of the time during this trying period of our lives.

I had been meeting with my mentor, Mrs. Par, and a lady prayer warrior in our church for a few years. She mentored me and became my best encouragement in reading God's Word, saying intercessory prayers, and worshipping. I would get calls from her weekly to get together for prayer at our church or at our home. Even when I'd try to tell her how busy I was, she would not take no for an answer. I'm glad she didn't, though. It was always worth my time. God was helping me grow closer to Him, even though times were tough. She actually asked me was I ready to go to war the first time we talked. Wow, she was such a prophetess and blessing to me.

I even had a ladies' breakfast Bible study for a year or so. I would stay up most of the night cleaning house and baking food or making breakfast for us all. God was really showing me His strength through my weaknesses. A reflection I had on this part of my life went like this:

Like David while tending sheep
I learned to praise and write poems
As I raised my little lambs
I fought battles of depression, loneliness, and self control
My lion and bears
I was trained, bold and ready
When my Goliath named Tragedy appeared
He came to provoke me with his taunts
He did not know how much God loved me
He had made a way for me
When my Goliath named Tragedy appeared
He laughed at me because I looked weak
All I had was one stone named Jehovah
I threw it upon my enemy
Although that stone seemed to move in slow motion
Down my adversary would go
What he meant for my destruction

> God would use for His Glory
> Now I carry around his head named Tragedy
> It is my testimony that I have the victory
> In The Name of the Lord and Heaven's Army
> **Lynn Payne**

With God's help I learned to fight off the depression and persevere. I began to put my family first and had to let go of some responsibilities at church and other activities I enjoyed. It was clear if I did not take control of my life and schedule, my peace would be gone. Most of all I wanted to be the wife and mother God would have me be.

This was around the year 2000. Jacob was about three.

I realized the house did not have to be perfect and neither did I nor did my family. I began to relax a little as a mother. I would let Jacob dress himself and play in the mud—things I would never have done with Blake and Leslie. He was the light in all of our lives anyway. We all spoiled and indulged him!

My husband started his own timber company in 2001. This seemed very exciting. I quit cleaning houses and would keep the company books. I did most of the work at home, but as it got more involved I began to work at our family office where my brothers also ran their company.

My mom and my good friend Cathy Mutvic had to help me learn to handle all the details. It was hard for me and began to be a lot to keep up with. When Blake and Leslie were at school, my sister-in-law Shelia would keep Jacob for me. I took him to work with me when Blake and Leslie could not help in the afternoons. It was okay; I had never had to leave my kids much for work, and I was just thankful that it was flexible, and I could be there for ballgames, appointments, et cetera. It gave me a heart for and more understanding of working moms.

You know it when the Lord is really real to you and preparing you for something. I was on a spiritual high those next few years. I was reading, studying, worshipping, and working for the Lord. In my naïveté, I even prayed, "Lord, use me! Please use me—whatever it takes."

By the year 2002 Blake was a junior in high school and Leslie was thirteen. Jacob was in K-4 and turned five in September. Our business was doing pretty well, and although the work was getting harder, we had cash flow. With Blake driving and with Jacob (my baby) going to school, things had slowed down a bit for me. Everything seemed good. I did not know it, but these would be our last few months together. Jacob was about to leave us for Heaven, so God could be glorified. His five years here on earth were coming to a close.

It was Christmas time. Jacob was all into it! He made me decorate the tree Thanksgiving night and was so excited to decorate the outside of the house with me and to take in everything about the wonder of Christmas. I tried to remind him about the real meaning of Christmas, but let's face it—for a five year old, it's all about the toys!

Jeff was notorious for getting the kids a huge, extravagant gift whenever their "year" came up . . . and this was Jacob's year! Jeff worked a lot that year. He did not shop until Christmas Eve. He said when he saw the four-wheeler, he knew that if they approved his credit, he would get it for Jacob. They did.

Surprise was the very core of Jeff's idea of Santa Claus, so the four-wheeler was top secret. We never even told the other siblings of the surprise. I usually did not even know what the big gift would be until the last minute.

We took communion with Jacob after we took a tour of "Bethlehem" at our church. It is a memory to cherish. We were to choose a ball ornament or a candy cane from the church Christmas tree. When I chose a ball ornament, Jacob, of course, had a meltdown! Whoever was there gave him a candy cane, and all was well again.

Christmas was a glorious morning. Jacob was so excited over the four-wheeler! Jeff said that Jacob's reaction to the gift made it all worth it that morning.

One night during the week before Christmas, I awoke. As I have mentioned, it had been very cold, and as I looked out the window I could see there was a heavy frost. The stars were so bright, I thought it had snowed. I walked outside in excitement, hoping for snow, but I realized it was the most beautiful starry night I had ever seen. I began impulsive, uninhibited praise for God for this beautiful gift He was giving me. I thought especially of how Mary traveled to Bethlehem on a night like this, so full of hope for her son to be born to save the world.

I was so touched by this whole season of Christmas; somehow, I felt I was part of a new story. I had the sense that a new chapter— containing what I did not know—was opening in our lives.

Of course, at the moment, I was not aware of any significance to it all. I was just honored that the Lord was sharing special things with me. I was thirty-three, the age Jesus was when he died.

I do not make this comparison lightly. I know I am no more special than anyone reading this. Yet I see significance in this loss at the age of thirty-three. If our lives are not tied to the Lord's, what else does anything matter? We suffer in this life for no other reason than to help us grow closer to our Creator and to help others who suffer. Jesus was a man of many sorrows. I love that about Him. It helps me bear mine.

I so wish I could comfort Jesus, but I realize all I do most of the time is let Him down. He's always there to catch me when I fall and to extend mercy and grace. Yet sometimes I soar in His strength. Of course, only through my weakness is that ever possible.

The week before Christmas was so very busy. Blake was having one of his last varsity basketball games before Christmas break. It was an out of town game, so as usual, we rode with my friend and cousin by marriage, Tammie, to the ballgame. Kolby, her thirteen-year-old son, who was Jacob's buddy, had us listen to a beautiful new song called "I Can Only Imagine." He had it on tape. Jacob and his sister and cousins were so loud in the car Tammie had to start it over several times. We would play this song later at Jacob's memorial service.

After all the ballgames, we always told Jacob that Blake's team won (even though they were on a losing streak then). He played with the other kids the whole time the game was on and didn't follow what was going on, so it was easy to convince him they won.

He'd say, "Yeah!" and run and play some more.

Once my friend, Pam Dunn, saw Jacob pulling on my leg and asking, "Did Blake's team win?"

Before I could answer, she told him, "No, honey, they lost."

Well, needless to say, it was another meltdown. Jacob was devastated. We comforted him while laughing with each other.

After a few moments of tears and anguish, he was back playing with his toys but he was still saddened. After all, Blake and his buddies were his heroes. They just had to win!

Life is so simple and precious when you enjoy it through the eyes of a child. One time Jacob wore his toy yellow construction goggles to one of Blake's games. He told me it was so he could see Blake real well, like he was wearing binoculars. He also had on fake gold medals and rubber boots.

Leslie would say, "Please don't let him go to the game dressed like that!"

But of course, I did. Whatever made him happy! It will be all right, I boasted as she rolled her eyes. And it was.

Leslie thought she was Jacob's mom more than his sister, which was fine with me. I needed all the help I could get! Although he was not so willing, she made him have photo sessions when I was at work and taught him school and Bible lessons. He would bargain with her to get his way.

He wrapped adults around his little finger all right! My uncle

Hank, who had never had kids of his own, had been a good uncle, doing things for and with Blake and Leslie. Yet when Jacob was born, it was different; he treated him like his own child. He came by at least once a week to see Jacob when he was a baby. I think they made their first excursion together when Jacob was still in diapers! Jacob always sat with him at church and asked him where they were going to go that day. This melted Hank's heart. Jacob loved him so much. Hank would let him pick out whatever candy he wanted at the store after church. They also started going to movies, the fair, the museum, and all kinds of exciting adventures. Somehow Jacob always had toys and treats when they got back! He would be exhausted too.

Hank had many plans for Jacob. He had not missed one of his T-ball games, and I'm sure he planned to be a part of whatever sport or activity Jacob enjoyed throughout school. After the accident, while waiting at the emergency room, someone said, "Has anyone called Hank?"

I was in such a state of shock I had not even thought of him. My heart sank for him. He told me later he was at work and some friends took him into an office and told him about the accident. I can't imagine what he was feeling.

After Jacob's death, there are years of family pictures where no one is smiling. We all look so solemn. Although the day would come when we could smile again, it took some time to feel like a family again for those of us he left behind.

A light in our lives had gone out.

Chapter Seven

Heaven and Hell on Earth

The night of Jacob's visitation was very cold, but in spite of that, many friends waited in a long line that wound around outside the funeral home. The Lord helped me that night as I greeted hundreds of friends and acquaintances. I was able to recall each one that came through the line; not one name escaped me. Every story shared, every card sent, every flower or gift given was so special.

I would walk over to Jacob in his casket every few minutes and just look at him or touch his hand. He was beautiful.

It was as if I was on auto-pilot. I was definitely in shock. I wasn't even crying. I stood till the last few people came through the line. You never know how strong you are until you do something like that.

While I was touched by every word and gesture made by each and every one who came to see Jacob in this hour, I was screaming inside. Deep underneath all the layers of shock, there was no denying I was still alive and able to feel. I knew a part of me had died with Jacob.

I was also worried about Blake and Leslie and what a terrible thing this was for them to go through. The kids—friends and cousins—spent the night with us again, so again the house was full of people. Some close friends were at the house also when I got home from the visitation, and we sat around the table, talking.

A layer of shock peeled off, and I began to feel something strongly. I wasn't angry, but I remember thinking, "I can't sit here and just talk like everything is fine. My life is over. My whole world has changed forever. They have no idea how I feel right now. They can't imagine."

Now, as I thought about it, I was absolutely convinced that I would never be happy again. It was so hard. It had all happened so suddenly. How could I face life on earth and my future here without my child? I really had not yet gone there in my mind—looked into the future, that is. The task of laying Jacob to rest had been enough to consume all my strength.

I got up to go to the bathroom and felt like it was all right not to go back. Jeff needed fellowship and that was good for him, but I was feeling mentally exhausted from it all.

I was determined to press on and have a beautiful memorial service the next day. I was still actively being Jacob's mama. Mama always finds the strength to do the motherly thing, even if it's to say goodbye.

We did have a beautiful service the next day.

As I mentioned, on the way to one of Blake's ball games, Jacob's cousin Kolby had played a new song for us called "I Can Only Imagine." Jacob and all the kids were so loud we had to play it twice to hear the lyrics. I will always believe that song was written just for us. It was the first time many people heard it when we played it at the service. The words are all about imagining what it will be like to go to Heaven and meet Jesus; whether a person will dance freely or be too in awe to move—will he shout hallelujah or be unable to speak at all? These are the lyrics to the song:

I Can Only Imagine
Bart Millard

Published by
Lyrics © MUSIC SERVICES, INC.

I can only imagine what it will be like
When I walk by Your side
I can only imagine what my eyes will see
When Your face is before me
Will I dance for You, Jesus
Or in awe of You be still

Brother Frank added special verses to "Jesus Loves Me" and "Twinkle, Twinkle, Little Star," and "All Night, All Day" which he and his sweet wife Mrs. Pam sang at the funeral in tribute to Jacob.

"Twinkle, Twinkle, Little Star, how I wonder what you are
Up above the world so high, like a diamond in the sky
Twinkle, Twinkle, little star, how I wonder what you are.

There's a new star hung in place, filled
with God's amazing grace
Up in heaven shining bright, with the love of Jesus' light

Twinkle, Twinkle, little man, resting in the Father's hand.

Jesus loves me, this I know, for the Bible tells me so
Little ones to him belong; they are weak but He is strong
Yes, Jesus loves me
Yes, Jesus loves me
Yes, Jesus loves me, for the Bible tells me so
Now I know His peaceful love for I'm living high above
all this world's defeat and harms
Safe in Jesus' loving arms.
All night, all day when I lay me down to
sleep, angels watchin' over me.
I pray the Lord my soul to take, angels watching over me.
All night, all day, angels watchin' over me, my Lord.
If I should die before I wake, angels watchin' over me, my Lord,
I pray the Lord my soul to take, angels watchin' over me.
Mommy, Daddy don't you fear, angels
watchin' over me, my Lord
I'll greet you when you make it here, angels watchin' over me.
Brother, sister when you come, angels watchin' over me,
I'll be playing at God's throne, angels watchin' over me."

Brother Frank also wrote a poem for Jacob called "Jacob's Special Day."

Jacob's Special Day

Who wakes up in the morning knowing what the day will hold?

Will the sun be shining brightly, will
the wind blow fierce and cold?
Is it a day to dig in the dirt or swing high in the sky?
Or celebrate a birthday or a day to question why?
Do tiny animals understand the joy that sunrise brings?
Does any mother know just how angels get their wings?
Every day begins, just like any other morn
When God swings out His hand and another child is born.
Another heart is filled with love and none of it is by chance.

It sometimes doesn't seem quite fair when angels come to call
and escort home another angel, added to their hall.
No, this day isn't like the rest, a peace for me has come
In my Father's mansion, a place that I call home.
It isn't like another day, and never again will be
But one day, friends and family, your faces I will see
So be brave and honest and every moment pray
This isn't just routine; it is my special day.

It was sweet and sorrowful all at once. There was some sense of joy and celebration amidst the sadness. Mixed with the sorrow, there was also peace that a pure and beautiful child was at rest in his eternal home and that someday there would be a reunion. But there were many dark days to come.

Ironically, the first funeral I ever remember attending was that of a little five-year-old boy, Jody Allgood. He was our neighbor, and we rode to school together. I remember the sick feeling in my stomach when I heard the news that Jody had died. My mother told me the morning after what had happened as she woke me for school the next day. I cried as I took a shower; tears fell with the water. The smells of fresh flowers as they die always reminds me of seeing the body of that little boy, just as the smell of the Giorgio perfume my cousin Dawn wore on the way to the funeral home makes me think of that first encounter I had with such a tragic death.

I took in everything about that experience when I was just eleven or twelve years old, seeing Mrs. Elaine Allgood lose her young child, and I never forgot it. I remember how the mother was so brave she even said words at her son's funeral. I remember how when we visited her house, she cried and held my brother, who was only a year or two older than her Jody. She asked my mother if it was all right to bury her son in the suit my mom had passed down to her from my brother. My mother said that of course it was, and Mrs. Allgood gave my brother a little car or something and told him he would have to come back to see her.

I remember how this grieving mother cared for her child's graveside with flowers and beautiful gardens and how she always seemed sad. She was my mom's cousin, and everyone in that family is very talented and creative.

The whole community grieved over that loss. I heard talk from the adults about how she held her child at the funeral home. Even kids at the school lunchroom talked about the sad things that happened that night when he died.

I just listened. I knew Jody. He was a full-blooded boy; he had go carts, toys, and everything a boy would want. One day he was there, riding to school with me and playing with my brothers, and the next he was gone.

I went on with my life, of course, but it still seems to me that from that point on, I was not a little girl anymore. I was realizing that life is not a fairy tale. Life can change at any moment. I did not understand how such a thing could happen, but I now knew it could.

I feel such a bond with her. We are women and mothers. We are strong and weak. We are creative and repressed. We are wiser than most. We don't take things for granted. We are survivors. She is actually my cousin and I am proud to share the same "Little" blood with her.

To this day I think she is one of the strongest women I know. She and her husband lived through the worst thing ever. He seemed to be her rock. Yet without him, after he died, she still survived. When she was widowed she still lived out in the country alone. I pray life and Heaven are especially kind to her.

She even had a flower shop that she ran out of her home. She did amazing work. She did my prom flowers. It is even more of a testimony to her strength and how she took something so horrible and used the pain to help others. She and her husband bought the funeral home in town, which was poorly run, and turned it into a respectable, well-run business. They did it so that others like me would not have to worry about our loved one's dignity at times of loss; our needs at such challenging times would be well taken care of by this beautiful woman. I even worked there for a while when I was a young mom.

She had eventually sold the funeral home to our friend, Harold Reece, Jr. Who worked for her. He continued to serve hurting, bereaved families with excellence also. I heard that the night Mrs. Allgood heard about Jacob's death, she did not sleep all night. I dread the day I hear of someone I know who is given this cross to bear.

Yet that is truly why I am writing this book, because this happens to someone every day. When and if something like this happens to you or something else grievous occurs—a loss you think you cannot endure—you must not give up. You must live. When I anticipated my first grandchild's birth, I was so glad I was alive, so glad I did not die of grief, even though sometimes I wanted to perish or die. I pray that you too will not die from your loss but will live. *Life will come again if you walk it out with God and all those you love. Do not give up.* No doubt you know the stories of the lost sheep and the lost coin. Jesus told these stories thousands of years ago, about how when a shepherd lost one sheep out of a hundred, he would leave the 99 that were safe in order to go find the missing one. Jesus followed that story with a similar one: we may have a pile of money, but if one coin is lost, we spend much time and energy searching for that one lost coin. We sorely miss what we have lost, and God is concerned about our losses too.

Jesus followed these two simple stories up with the story of the prodigal son—the lost son who returned home after leaving to live a wasteful and sinful life. This story is relevant today too. Many people have prodigal children—lost children—teenagers and young adult children, even older adult children who, for one reason or another, abandon their parents' values and wander dark paths. Sometimes those children are permanently lost, sometimes they come back. Some die from addictions or in violent circumstances related to their rebellion or they just never come back in heart, and there is estrangement for many decades.

Those who have prodigal children may understand something of what it is like to lose a child. Some prodigals don't leave home, but they are still gone. They are strangers; your sweet, obedient younger child has "died." Such prodigals disrespect and ignore their parents in their own homes. This is very sad and painful. You pray they will return to their senses, and you struggle with how to deal with your loss.

In the Bible the father sees the prodigal son coming back from a long way off. I've heard it interpreted that this means the father was gazing up the road when anyone approached, probably hoping against hope that one of those times it would be his long lost son, coming home. Then one day it was, and the father rejoiced, saying say his son "was dead and is alive again" (Luke 15: 32). As long as a child lives, there is hope he or she will "come home" again, "live" again.

A dead child cannot be retrieved physically. There is a gulf. You cannot reach out and lay your hands on him or her again. He or she doesn't appear from a long way off the road, approaching home again. A deceased child is gone—and that word "gone" takes on a whole new meaning when you are dealing with the physical death of a child. There will be no tearful return, no finding of what was lost, no restoration of the wayward son to his place of prominence in a family.

Yet in many ways, there is divine restoration or retribution . . . poetic justice, you could say. As I've mentioned, many parts of Jacob's life and spirit have shone through in our lives, with my son Blake becoming a preacher and my granddaughter Anslee having so much of Jacob's personality and spirit. That which is lost can return, maybe in unexpected ways (and there is much rejoicing in Heaven and on earth when that which was lost is found).

I often say I grieved the best years of my life away. From the age of thirty-three to forty-three is a blur of grief and battle after battle. God has given Jeff and me some wonderful times together lately, and I feel strong and very energetic again for the Lord's work. I think this is another way of saying God will give you beauty for ashes. (Isaiah 61).

You will find something after your loss too. You will gain something. You will come back full even though you left empty. If you are like me, you will find that every wound and scar turns into a mark of the Holy Spirit in your soul. That is precious beyond measure.

As Jacob's earthly mother, after his death I felt the fact that he was gone physically so strongly, I wondered sometimes how I could keep on living. That New Year's Day, with the funeral over, the body laid to rest, with pictures and memories displayed, all I could think was, "My God, my God, why have You forsaken me?"

That cry from Jesus at His last helped me. I knew that Jesus was the king of pain, and that was the only reason I could even think of going on. David, a man after God's own heart, actually said the words first.

There was such a great gulf between me and my child and, for all my longing, I could not reach across that bottomless chasm and touch him, nor could he come back to me. As it says in Luke 16:26: "Between us and you there is a great gulf fixed, so that those who want to pass from here to you cannot, nor can those from there pass to us."

Even my name seemed to echo back to me my new reality: Lynn Payne, or "Pain". It seemed that was who I was now and who I was always going to be.

Yet pain isn't the problem. Pain is the symptom. I sometimes thought I was going to die of my pain, that my sorrow would result in some terminal illness. In my heart, I knew I was already dead. I didn't even want anyone to help me. I wanted them to let me die.

Depression literally means to be pressed down, and when that happens, you are squeezed down so low, you are out of balance within. You get out of sync on the physical and emotional levels, and you must try to get it back in balance so you can stand high again with God. It is not easy. It was not easy for me.

I concentrated on knowing I would be reunited with Jacob one day in the spiritual world, in Heaven, in eternity. I knew that Jacob still existed in a special place with God, and that was a great comfort and a reunion to which to look forward. My son was not lost from me forever. Far from it. We would meet and embrace again.

Heaven was up front now in all my thoughts and in my imagination. Funny how I never thought much about Heaven as a real, 24-7 place before. After Jacob's death, I wanted to learn everything about Heaven and a person's journey from earth to Heaven when they die. I want to imagine everything that happened that sunny afternoon, when for whatever reason, My Lord chose to allow Jacob's guardian angel to step aside and Jacob entered Heaven there, from the red clay of Georgia, after that awful accident.

Meanwhile, I had to live out my life on earth, where the joys of motherhood had turned into sorrow, and each colorful reminder of Jacob in our home, from clothing left behind to happy memories of his voice and laughter, only brought with them the most gut-wrenching pain I have ever endured or thought I would have to endure. The body blows of sorrow literally took my breath away; there were many times when I could hardly gasp in air. I spent much of my time sighing, groaning, with no peace, no rest—only pain, anxiety, and upheaval.

I was like Job: "For my sighing comes before I eat, and my groanings pour out like water. For the thing I greatly feared has come upon me, and what I dreaded has happened to me. I am not at ease, nor am I quiet; I have no rest, for trouble comes" (Job 3:24-26).

We got through it. We were put into the refining fire, and sure enough, what came out ended up to be beauty after the pain, gold after the impurities were burned out. We came through the smothering dark tunnel of sorrow and found the light and air on the other side.

This is how I know that whatever your loss, you can get through it too.

You may ask, "How can one live with a broken heart?"

You can, because God feels your pain as much or more than you do, and He will move to save you. The Bible says, "The LORD is near to those who have a broken heart, and saves such as have a contrite spirit" (Psalm 34:18), and "He heals the brokenhearted and binds up their wounds" (Psalm 147:3).

You can live with a broken heart because of this one reason: God is close to the brokenhearted.

Chapter Eight

Left Behind

As I've mentioned, I always had struggled in school and felt insecure in academic-type things, but that was okay because I was able to be a wife and mom. I had considered that being a good mother was my highest calling, and I wanted to be the kind of mother God wanted me to be. It was all I ever dreamed of, growing up: having a great family. By the grace of God, I met a man from a wonderful family, and marriage seemed to be everything of which I dreamed. To top off my marital happiness, I had a boy and a girl, and while we were building our dream home, I found out I was pregnant with another baby, Jacob.

Yet being a wife and mother is no small task; it is very hard. By nature, I am pretty high strung and nervous. I was ever aware of my weaknesses, but I so desired to be used spiritually.

2 Corinthians 12:9 was and remains my life verse: "My grace is sufficient for you, for My strength is made perfect in weakness." That verse has come true for me, almost jumping off the page to become a part of my daily life.

I admit I still have some really anxious moments, and I'm still not very wise in book smarts or technology, so please don't think I'm bragging about my Christian faith. I'm not.

Yet I have to say that I believe this terrible thing that happened—the loss of my beloved baby—has been the way He has chosen to answer my prayer to be used in whatever way He willed for me. I do realize that in the midst of all the sorrow and pain, I have received from Him a special gift of compassion and love for hurting people. I feel like this has softened my hard edges. It has helped me not focus so much on this world but on eternity. Those are precious gifts indeed.

In 2 Corinthians 5:6 it says that "while we are at home in the body we are absent from the Lord." Jacob's death made me yearn to be away from the body and live in the world of the spirit, as he was doing.

This verse was on my refrigerator when Jacob died: Romans 12:2: "And do not be conformed to this world, but be transformed by the renewing of your mind, that you may prove what is that good and acceptable and perfect will of God." I could not be conformed to this world when someone so dear to me was taken out of it. This world, to me, was a vale of tears and a reminder of loss, so latching my eyes onto eternity, to a better and higher world where there were peace and happiness and the things of God seemed a natural result.

God has placed a yearning for eternity in the human heart, but when your child is there, your heart is surely there too, in ways you never imagined before. You want to go there too, right away, to be with your child.

You don't even have visitation rights—you just get glimpses of Heaven on earth. You have the occasional dream or vision. Also, I would search for clues in God's words about Heaven. I sought out chances for communication through signs and wonders. Around the house, I was always searching for that which was left behind, and I found things.

Left behind were my husband, my health, my other children, and my church. I had so much, and there was still so much ahead. I would ask God, "Don't let me let go," and beg Him to hold onto me when I tried to let myself go.

In time I would have to renew my desires for everything left behind, even though, in comparison to eternity and reunion with my youngest child, it did not seem so desirable anymore.

Every day I had to fight to hold onto my sanity because the days and years following Jacob's death were nothing short of all out war against my whole family. Each day seemed to hold a new battle. We suffered so much. There was so much stress, so much conflict. So much additional sorrow came along as we staggered under the weight of our terrible bereavement and the happiness it had stolen away from those of us who were left behind. I truly believed I would never be happy again. That is the lie with which the devil kills so many.

I wanted to die. I begged God to let me die.

People would say, "You're so strong."

In fact, I was brokenhearted to be left behind on this earth without my Jacob.

Still God breathed life into me with each task and test we faced. I will never forget how close God was to me in those days. I actually miss it sometimes, it was so intense and His presence was so real.

When you are thrown up against the ropes, fighting an opponent who is much stronger than you are, ready to throw in the towel, call on Him. That is when you will feel the real power of God. That is when you will see His intervention. Then somehow, beyond all hope and understanding, you will wind up standing in the middle of the ring, your foe gone, and you still on your feet. You may be bruised. You may be bloody. You may be forever changed. You can stand in His strength even though your knees may be shaking, you are standing up. It is a miracle.

If you have ever seen the Disney movie *The Lion King*, there is a part where the little lion Simba, who will someday grow up to be the lion king, is cornered by a pack of hungry hyenas. They are intent on eating the little king-to-be. Simba tries to roar like he's seen his father, Mufasa, the full-grown lion king, do. Of course, he sounds like a little baby squeaking. Then, suddenly, a huge, growling, terrifying roar is heard, seemingly coming out of his little mouth. He turns around and sees it is Mufasa behind him. He has come in the nick of time to rescue his adventurous little cub.

I sometimes feel like that is the way it is when we are fighting the enemy. Our only real weapon is our free will. If we choose to turn to God in praise, prayer, and worship, our baby squeaks turn into something serious—a mighty roar—and we are saved, rescued by the lion that is God. He always has our backs, lending His strength to our weakness.

This is what David must have meant when he said in Psalms 40:2: "He also brought me up out of a horrible pit, out of the miry clay, and set my feet upon a rock, and established my steps."

If you have been sunken into a miry pit, with blinding mud in your eyes, and your hands all scratched and bleeding from trying to climb out on your own power, call on Him. Tell Him you can't see, you can't climb, you can't get out of it yourself; you feel helpless. Ask Him to take your hand and tug you out. I guarantee that He will do it. He will send a glimmer of light so you can see beyond the mud and mire; He will clasp your hand and haul you out of any pit or quicksand you fell into. He will do that for you. He did it for me.

If you are facing inconsolable loss, you must persevere in faith that there is One who sees, One who cares, One who knows it all. Grieve, by all means. Believe me, I did. Grief became the full-time occupation of my family and me. I assure you, it was the hardest work I had ever done, just holding on when grief was so overwhelming, the desire to give up so strong, just wanting to wallow in sorrow and not have to gather up the strength to pick up the broken pieces and try to build something new out of them again. It seemed easier just to stay sunken down into despair.

You have to be very careful because the darkness of grief can be very addictive. It can be dangerous because of the emotion involved. Always pray to God to help you know when it is time to stop crying, when it is time to stop listening to sad music to as you grieve, and when it is time to stop spending time alone.

Also, pray constantly not to become bitter. No matter what has happened to you, there is always something to be thankful for. Some say it helps to stay busy; others do better to rest and pamper themselves. Find what helps you. Do take a moment to notice when and if your tears are ones of self-pity, and ask God to help you with that too. That kind of grieving really doesn't help. God can always point you to someone who needs your help. My children were what kept me going because they needed me. But I realize some have lost their only child or children. I still try to do things for others who are in need. That helped me so much.

We can also realize that God, who sees every sparrow, not only grieves with you over your loss; He is grieving with people all over the world over their losses too.

I just had to take it one day at a time, especially at holidays and parties. It is true that time helps, but only God can heal. The kind of pain you experience when you lose a child is so deep, only God can touch that wound with healing grace. Only God can penetrate that profoundly into the hurting human soul. Only God really knows how you feel.

I had to have confidence that God left me behind for a reason. Maybe it was to tell you, dear reader, that He loves you and He has a divine destiny and plan for your life.

I had to tell God that it was okay that He had left me behind, that I understood that I'd eventually be okay and even happy again here on earth. Time was to prove that was true, but it was difficult to believe for a long while that I would ever, ever be happy again after being so bereft and left behind.

Chapter Nine

Guilt, Forgiveness, and "Why, Lord, Why?"

Whenever something bad happens in our lives, I think the first question that pops into a person's mind is: "Why? Why me? What did I do to deserve this? Why was I chosen to be the one to have this happen? Why is So-and-So over there doing so well, while I must suffer this tremendous loss?" I have found some answers that have consoled me. I hope anyone who grieves finds the answer to their questions: "Why, Lord, why? Why me?"

I could not have found it or made it on my path without faith. I must say, the people of my faith community were very instrumental in my healing. It is tempting to miss church, meetings, and activities when you feel sad and defeated, but I found it is good for you and for others for you to get out.

Some events will bring you pain, so be prepared for that. The first Easter without Jacob was so hard for me. As I've mentioned, I felt sad as I looked at all the young children in their pretty, new Easter clothes and wondered why my child had to die.

I tried to focus on Jesus and the meaning of the day, but for the most part I failed to do so and thought mostly about my own pain.

While I was grateful for Jesus' sacrifice, I was struggling awfully hard with my own.

I pushed myself, though. Jeff and Leslie and I were in the Easter drama, and I was on edge the whole week before as to how I was going to have the strength to get through it. We had to perform it on Friday, Saturday, and Sunday nights.

Jeff and I got into a big fight the Saturday before Easter Sunday as we were on the way to one of Blake's ball games. I told Jeff he hadn't been there for me lately. I felt that he did not carry as heavy a burden as I—the mother—did and that he needed to support me more emotionally. Jeff let me know in no uncertain terms that he was struggling too when he screamed, "I lost my son too!" Well, I certainly heard that. The argument was over then, followed just by silence and tears. I was sorry for Jeff and mad at him all at the same time.

I have heard there is an ancient story from the Orient about a husband and wife who lose a child to death. The mother weeps a great deal and talks about it all the time (as Leslie and I approached our healing after Jacob's death). The father is silent all the time (as Jeff and Blake tended to be). Finally, the mother can't stand her husband's silence any longer, and she breaks down and screams at him over the dinner table. She accuses him of not caring. He still says nothing, but when he opens his mouth blood comes out. That is how much he is feeling inside. He is bleeding internally from the stress of his sorrow.

I realized during that fight that Jeff was hurting as much as I was—he just dealt with it in a different way. I never meant to make it all about me. It's just that it is especially hard to let go after you've carried someone in your womb. Bone of my bone and flesh of my flesh applies so strongly to the mother of a child. If a child doesn't get enough calcium from the mother's diet while he is in the womb, calcium will be taken from the mother's own teeth and bones to be given to the child. When you've had that deep a relationship with someone, nurturing them with the very stuff of your bones and teeth, it is hard—it is extremely hard—to let go. Your baby has been a part of you, literally. That which was a part of you has been ripped away. Sometimes I say that grace was my skin at that time, because my whole being was so raw and exposed from having had my baby torn from my arms and taken away from my earthly life.

The Easter drama was a success. I could see before my eyes and know in my heart how many lives were touched by the story of Jesus' life and death. I had many moments when I thought I couldn't possibly get through the play, but I felt from the start Jesus was telling me to persevere and was giving me strength, and that is why I made it.

I loved the part when I followed Jesus with the other ladies to the cross. Dressed in black, with my head covered, I felt it was very natural and poetic for me to play this part.

That Easter was, as is typical, stressful getting us all dressed up and to church on time. I also had baskets to make for others. Blake and Leslie and I snapped at each other and got into an argument on the way to church. I hate the devil even more so when I give in to him and show anger and unfairness. We were all crying by the time we got to church. I apologized, and we went inside.

I was so grateful for my faith community. Some people whom I barely knew reached out and touched my life, bringing me the exact antidote I needed for my grief at that moment.

One kind lady from Jacob's school, Paula Warnock, brought me a book right after Jacob died that she said she was reading at the time of the accident. That fact made her realize that the book was more for me than for her. She was right. The book was perfect for me, and I will explain why. It was about John the Baptist and his struggle with the final moments of his life and how Jesus sees our struggles.

Matthew 11 tells us that when John the Baptist was in prison waiting for his execution, he sent a message to Jesus and asked, "Are You the Coming One, or do we look for another?" (Matthew 11:3). Jesus told his disciples to go witness to John about the miracles he had performed, making the blind see and the lame walk.

He added, "And blessed is he who is not offended because of Me" (Matthew 11:6).

John the Baptist knew Jesus was the Messiah; he had proclaimed him. John also knew that he himself was only the forerunner. He had preached to his disciples that he must decrease so Jesus could increase, yet in his flesh he struggled with the question of whether Jesus was the true one or not.

Jesus was not offended by John's human weakness and doubt. He would pray about his own destiny at Gethsemane, asking if this cup could possibly be taken away from him. He still bowed to God's will if that was not to be possible.

From this I gleaned that Jesus is not upset when we ask why things are as they are. God can understand that we would have liked things to have turned out differently. If we ask respectfully, not blaming God (even though I think He understands that too and waits gently for us to overcome it), I think God is willing to furnish us with reasons for our sufferings. At the very least He does not judge us for wondering why things had to be this way.

Job asked why. Job didn't know that God had suggested this test for him. His confusion is understandable, as is ours. As long as we ask in faith and with open minds, I think God is ready, willing, and able to answer any questions we have. He may even want to answer all our "Whys" in order to help set our feet more firmly on our paths. He waits.

John knew all about Jesus even from before birth, when he leaped in his mother's womb as Elizabeth approached the pregnant Mary. Yet his feelings were hurt by what he had to endure. John did not know that at this very time of his struggles Jesus was proclaiming that there was never a greater man born of woman than John the Baptist (Matthew 11:11).

John the Baptist saw the Spirit of God descending like a dove on Jesus and heard the voice of God saying, "This is my beloved Son, in whom I am well pleased" (Matthew 3:17). He had great favor with

God. I can relate to John the Baptist's struggles and how hard it was then to endure what he was given to bear.

If such a one could have his doubts when the reality of death was upon him, I think God understands when we also have our doubts and our fears and hard times believing this is the will of God when the big challenges come our way. I imagine He understands when we weep and wail and ask: "Why, Lord? Why?"

I know I had favor with God before the tragedy. I had said, "God, use me, whatever it takes," but still my feelings were hurt when I met my destiny. It hurt more than I ever imagined. I wanted to scream: "I change my mind! Don't use me this way! God, how could you do this to me?"

I had thought I was special. I had worked so hard at church cleaning, praying, and studying with my prayer mothers, working with my girls' groups, children's church, Bible schools, and so on. I tried hard to be a good servant of God.

How could I have deserved what I was handed to deal with? I even reminded God about how I was always picking up all the kids for children's church and Wednesday night Bible study and taking them to church camp. I tried so hard to be a good member of the community, a good woman of faith and duty.

"This is how You thank me," I said to Him.

All this is not to mention how protective a mom I was, with all my rules and regulations. I had been a stay-at-home mom with my first two and did house cleaning and babysitting to help out financially. When Jacob was small, I cleaned two houses and the church so I was able to work around Blake's sports schedule and also car pool. I started doing the paperwork for Jeff's timber company in 2001, but I used our family office and could work my own schedule so I could be there for my children.

I took a lot of pride in being a good mother. To then lose a child because of one simple, mistaken decision was pretty ugly. Yet that one choice I made to let Jacob stay when Blake called changed everything. I did not even base it on correct information. When I said yes, I forgot they had gone down to his uncle's (my cousin's) that morning. I was thinking they were at my house, and Jacob would be safer at home.

All I would have had to say was, "No, bring him to me," but I didn't.

I had to learn not to be angry at God, not to be bitter over my fate, and to trust His plan. It took time and a lot of work.

I had to learn not to be angry at myself too. I had to forgive myself for making a decision any mother might have made on any typical day. I had to fight this almost every day—the guilt, the self-blame. How could I have let this happen? If it wasn't my fault, it had to be someone's fault, like Adam said in the garden that the fall was all Eve's fault or even deeper, that this was God's fault for giving Adam this woman.

I admit I was very bitter. Why was my child taken? Why did it have to be my Jacob? Why did it have to be me who suffered the loss of a child? I knew many other children who had been in lots more dangerous situations throughout the years, and they had come out just fine. Why didn't my Jacob come out of his dangerous situation just fine—a little bruised, a little broken, but still alive?

I spent hours tracing everything that had happened leading up to the accident and thinking how so many small things could have stopped it: just a different word here, just a different twist or turn there. Yet none of those small things happened.

Why didn't they?

This helped me to realize God let it happen, even though we all had a part in how that day played out. I struggled and told God: "You could have stopped this. Why didn't You? Where was Jacob's guardian angel?"

It was just so painful. I wanted my baby back. Reminders of him were everywhere in our house: his toys, his clothes, his smell, his spirit. In every room memories of him flooded my mind constantly. I cried. I cried. I screamed for him. I wanted our life back. I wanted my baby back. The longing I had for my child made me sick to my stomach. I came to know the real meaning of the word "lamentations" for lamenting was all I seemed to do.

Home was a dead zone. There was no laughter. Our baby was gone, and I felt like we had absolutely been robbed. It was as if everybody in the family was lost, not just Jacob. It was as if we had all lost our lives.

When I see pictures of us back then, it hurts to see the expressions on our faces. We had lost our smiles. We look so solemn, so stricken. Each one was drowning in his or her own grief. As I mentioned, some of us talked about it often (the girls) and some held it all in (the guys). Both were without balance.

This was uncharted territory. I had no experience of death like this. I had only lost my ninety-year-old Granny, who had led a full and long life. I didn't know how to do this.

I searched for books on grief and went to counseling. My life was about survival, not living. I feared and believed it would always be like this. I just wanted to die and go to Heaven instead of having to hang on to a life I no longer wanted, by my fingernails, as if I were dangling over a cliff.

When the accident first happened, I felt strong. I was carried by the Holy Spirit. I felt that God was in control of a bigger plan. As time went by, I had to constantly remind myself of this truth. Romans 8:28 says, "And we know that all things work together for good to those who love God, to those that are the called according to His purpose." Yet as time went on, my strength did not come to me as easily as it did at first. I had to fight for it. I began to seek the Holy Spirit like never before because I was aware of the battle I was in; that we were in; fighting for mental and emotional survival after one part of our family was ripped away from us, leaving a big, open, gaping wound we never thought would stop hurting or would heal.

I thank God for my Pentecostal roots. When you've been taught things of the spirit all your life, it comes back to you when you need it. When you are in great travail, all the wonderful things that have been poured into your soul and consciousness through church attendance, hymns, listening to beautiful music, studying the Word—they come forth and sustain you. If you have lived a life of faith, all the teachings kick in, and you almost go on automatic pilot to find your comfort in all the grace and wisdom that has been packed into your soul.

For example, the very first morning after Jacob's funeral, I woke up singing a song of praise. It was a simple little praise song of some sort. I can't even remember what the words were. The simplicity of the message was all I could handle. Those few little simple words were a comfort to my breaking heart. Also the book *Grace for the Moment* by Max Lucado and a book of poems a friend gave me were gentle messages that comforted me. You can't handle heavy material at this time.

I survived through knowing such things of God, even when it took all my effort just to keep breathing. My life was helped through a simple practice of saying, "Good morning, Holy Spirit," which I took from Benny Hinn's book that I had read years earlier. It was called *Good Morning, Holy Spirit.* I could never have made it through without the help of the Spirit that lives in each of us. There is power in the Holy Spirit. He was my Comforter. It is the supernatural ability inside of you that helps you to overcome. It is nearly impossible without it. I could not have made it without the Holy Spirit in my life after the loss of my son.

Many people can recall the day they were saved, but I cannot. I've heard preachers say that if you can't remember making that decision, you must not be saved. I disagree. They even say that if you sin, you must not have been truly saved. That may be their story—their truth—but it is not mine. I know I am saved. Shame on us for making the Gospel so hard! I have asked Him into my heart countless times.

However, I do recall when I was filled with the Holy Spirit. I was not particularly seeking, but as a young teen I was filled with the Holy Spirit with the evidence of speaking in tongues in a South Georgia Youth Camp prayer line. I received the baptism easily, with a child-like faith. The anointing was very strong in that moment and I also believe having witnessed so many genuine manifestations of the Spirit in my life also helped me receive it at that time.

Everyone's story is unique and different. I don't recall many more experiences speaking in my prayer language until I was a young mom. Yet the Holy Spirit has always been with me even when I put Him in the background or on the back burner.

I've always heard that He is a gentleman, and this is so true. He does not force Himself on anyone and He will wait patiently for you. If you are saved, He is with you, even if you have not experienced your prayer language. You may even be backsliding, but He is waiting to renew your heart. He is just waiting for your invitation. He is too gentle and gentlemanly to do otherwise.

In the Bible after David sinned, he prayed for the Lord to create in him a new heart and restore to him the joy of His salvation. His prayers were answered, and yours will be likewise.

I said all of that to bring you, the reader, to the place in my story where I realized that the Holy Spirit had prepared me for the events of my son's accident and my journey without him.

The Lord once spoke to me while I was in prayer: "I would comfort those who mourn." I remembered in the Beatitudes: "Blessed are those who mourn, for they shall be comforted" (Matthew 5:4).

A song, a few words, a phrase or sentence from the Bible can be a balm on the soul strafed by grief. A memory that seems to speak to you that you were somehow prepared for this, can help you realize that you may have a calling that will grow out of this loss you are suffering. May I comfort someone in some simple way! That's my job now. It's not a job I would have chosen, but it is the work before me. I pray to be a vessel used for God's glory.

I was not the perfect choice of someone who could overcome such a tragedy. I didn't have any kind of platform to reach out to people so that I could overcome it all and bring Him glory. As I've mentioned, I was already a person who struggled mentally.

I've noticed that God often chooses imperfect people. For example, there is Moses in the Bible, with his stutter. Why would God choose such a person to be his main leader and spokesman—someone who had to go into the court of the king and present his case? Moses even had to bring his brother Aaron with him for support because Moses stuttered so much. Still Moses led the people to the Promised Land. He was the right choice for the job.

Paul also seemed like an odd person to be the main conveyor of the Christian message to the ancient world. He was a persecutor of Christians! He too was the right one.

It happens over and over again in the Bible that God chooses unlikely people to be His instruments. I hope to be a small instrument of God who can perhaps bring comfort to those who have suffered losses, even though I am an unlikely choice for the job.

That has become my reason why.

As I mentioned, one of my dear friends told me I was the most romantic person she ever knew. Is that why I was chosen to endure this tragedy and come out of the smothering tunnel of sorrow to blink in the sunlight on the other side? Maybe. I do believe life is a romance. Indeed, the love relationship between us and our Creator should be reflected in everything we do. It should be reflected when we dance, when we hold our infant children up close as we sing or play a sweet lullaby or when we finish the words of a sentence for our beloved spouse. These moments are the loving ones in the gift of life that we treasure, and they should all be shared with God.

Maybe I am romantic enough to make a love story of my life with God and my family, even if that romance is tempered by profound loss. It is bitter turning to bittersweet until finally there is just the sweetness of the fond and loving memories and the flowers in our hearts grown from the watering of our tears.

Friends and family were indispensable to my healing too. A dear friend, Sonya Anderson, sent me many small gifts, just as little comforts for the pain she knew I was going through. I would send her back prayers. This is one of her letters to me, and you can feel how her heart broke with mine.

To Lynn, From Sonya:

I got your card. My heart just broke at the pain you and your family are in. I pray for you a lot. You know, life just isn't fair sometimes, but God knows what He is doing. I know you miss your baby, more than I can imagine, but God needed him for some reason. You just take one day at a time, one minute at a time. I love you, and I know we don't live near each other but I feel so close to you. One day soon we'll all be together in Heaven and you can hold him once again. But Lynn, he is so happy that you wouldn't want to bring him back. God knows your family's pain, and he is only a breath away.

I hope you liked the shirt I sent you. Just a little something to make you feel good."

Others like my brother, Mark, and cousin, Dawn, were always bringing me sweet gifts, like worship CDs, et cetera. My cousin Dawn even gifted me with a priceless painting of Jacob. My brothers covered the funeral expenses, and Jeff's brother bought the plot for burial for our whole family. Such words and deeds of comfort and understanding meant so much.

In 2014, a little more than a decade after Jacob's death, my anguished cry of "Why, Lord, Why?" had softened. I think you will see that in the song-like poem I wrote for Him:

Why, Lord?

Why, Lord?
I tried so hard and still I have failed

But I had hoped with Your help I could
Why do they hurt me?
Why do I do the things I do?
It seems that those who oppose me prosper
But I put my hope in You
Deliver me according to Your tender mercies
Not my will but Yours be done
Because I know I am Yours and You are mine
I am Yours ...You are mine
I am Yours ...You are mine

O, when I am down and when I am low
Heaven knows, Heaven knows
You are mine and I am Yours
You are mine and I am Yours

Why, Lord?
Why didn't they just see you were God?
You tried to show them
It would seem like they won
But You knew who You were
You could have come off that tree
If it hadn't been for me
Why would You do that for me?
Because I am Yours and You are mine
I am Yours ...You are mine

Lynn Payne

I am Yours ...You are mine

O, when I am down and when I am low

Heaven knows, Heaven knows

You are mine and I am Yours

You are mine and I am Yours.

Lynn Payne

Chapter Ten

Death's Shadow and
Life's Sunshine

I wandered through life in a fog after Jacob's death, wondering when it would lift. Everything was hazy.

I went to Blake and Leslie's school functions, I went through the motions of being their mother, and I tried to look forward to something. Yet the heaviness of the fog dimmed my view. I didn't want to cheat them; they'd already lost enough. I wanted to be there for them, but I couldn't shake the fog.

I thought, "I can't do anything to help Jacob, but I can help them. Help me, Lord. I don't want to let them down."

My heart's desire at the time was simply that we would survive as a family. I hoped, too, that somehow we would learn to give God the glory. To prosper and bless one another would be even better.

Sometimes those hopes seemed to be utterly in vain. I wondered how I would possibly have the strength to go on when I was so weak and broken in heart. I was able to wait on the Lord to renew my strength and to someday bring joy again. The joy of the Lord was my strength. In my weakness, His strength was made perfect.

I remembered Bible quotes such as Isaiah 26:3: "You will keep him in perfect peace, whose mind is stayed on You, because he trusts in You." When I wondered where I could put my hope, what I could put my hope in, the answer was always that my hope was only in God.

Sometimes my longing for Jacob was so great, I felt like an exile on this earth. I felt homesick for a country I had never been to before—sweet Beulah Land, as it says in the hymn by Edgar Page Stites:

> O Beulah land, sweet Beulah land!
> As on thy highest mount I stand,
> I look away across the sea
> Where mansions are prepared for me
> And view the shining glory shore
> My heaven, my home forever more.

When the Hebrews were exiled to Babylon from Jerusalem, they were promised a return in Isaiah 62:4: "You shall no longer be termed Forsaken, nor shall your land any more be termed Desolate; But you shall be called Hephzibah (My delight in in her), and your land Beulah (married)."

As the Hebrews would return from exile in Babylon to live their romance of being married to the will of God, perhaps I would return from my exile to be happy again too. I did not expect it to happen on this side of eternity, though.

How I longed for sweet Jesus. How I longed for sweet Jacob. How I longed and longed, especially as time went on. At two years, I had not seen him or held him for all that time, and I ached to do so even as I was still praying, fighting to be a good mom for Blake and Leslie, struggling to breathe, battling to keep going through the pain.

I couldn't wait to get to eternity where I would see Jacob every day. He was my sonshine in Heaven, whereas Leslie and Blake were my sunshine on earth. How we long for our children.

We lose them every step of the way. When they outgrow their little clothes, we put the clothes away regretfully. The child who was will never be again. Yes, we have a new, bigger child, with an ever-developing brain and personality, but our little one is gone, never to return except in pictures and memories.

There are many losses along the road of motherhood, of parenthood—when you see them off to school and surrender them to strangers and peers; when they earn their licenses and drive off . . . the first time they defy you . . . the first time they tell you they don't agree with you or maybe don't even like you.

We lose our children a little bit every day. I just lost my little one all at once, in one staggering blow, instead of all the small ones.

It was as if a part of me was ripped away and I had to stand there, raw, aching, feeling every wind with searing pain. Healing took a long time. Grace was my skin.

Yet slowly, slowly, I did heal.

Holidays and anniversaries are hard when you are grieving a loss. It is time when you are supposed to be joyful, and the contrast with what you are really feeling is great. A time of sunshine becomes one of shadow. It is time, though, to get to the real meaning of the holidays or anniversaries in a deeper way.

Jacob had not been in school after Christmas, so he never had school parties to make Valentine's Day cards. That particular holiday should have been easier because of that, but it wasn't. I took a rose to his graveside on Valentine's Day, telling him I wished I could do more. I said I would have cooked something special for him if he was here. Jeff got him a balloon and let it go a few days later. I sent an extra balloon and I let it go at the house a few days later and watched it as it disappeared. I kissed it before Jacob got it.

I hoped Jacob somehow heard or saw our attempts to communicate with him, the things we did to try to feel connected to him. Hank, his uncle, took a football to the graveside with a note to him. We've all had dreams that have comforted us. Nothing took the pain away, but each thing we thought of and tried somehow did make it a little more bearable.

I dreaded my first Mother's Day without Jacob, and I prayed for God to help me to focus on my mother and grandmother and Jeff's. Of course, I did not forget I was still Blake and Leslie's mother, and Jacob's mother still too. I was grateful to God for giving me that honor.

Some days the pages of the books of our lives are not so lovely. As I know, some days are just tragic. We must accept and live with it all, the sunshine and the shadow. The Amish make quilts called "Sunshine and Shadow" quilts. Each square is two triangles—one in black and one in a bright color. The effect is very graphic—life is composed of sunshine and shadow. In the end, the result can be beautiful, but if we expect it all to be sunshine, we are doomed to be disappointed.

That was one thing I learned after Jacob died—one thing I had to accept and which I have come to have peace about—is the fact that we live in a fallen world. Bad things happen. So many things are broken and get broken, almost beyond repair. There is a great deal of sorrow and suffering in this world.

Yet in this broken and sorry world, there are still wonderful things. How beautiful are friendships and family relations and the church body when we are there for each other in the good times and the bad.

Blake wrote an essay in college that talked about sorrow and loss, along with victory and gain. His professor was intrigued by it.

> Many people would say your high school years are the best time of your life, so cherish them while they last. I would definitely agree with that statement. My high school years had many ups and downs. My favorite times were spending time with family and friends and most definitely—football!

There is no sport that can even compare to football. For many who grow up in the South, it is a lifestyle. I grew up watching football and dreaming of being my favorite player. Then before I knew it, I was all grown up and doing what I had dreamed of doing ever since I could remember. I had worked so hard, lifted weights, and put so much time into what I loved, and finally I was going to get the chance to show everyone what I could do.

The lights were on, the stands were filling up, and I had chill bumps running down my spine.

Yet before the start of my senior year, my life suffered a big turnaround. Jacob, my five year old brother, was killed in an ATV accident. I dedicated my last year, my senior year of football, to Jacob. He loved it when Friday nights came around and he got to come to the school and watch me play. All he wanted was to be just like me when he grew up. He loved sports, and his favorite sport was football. So when my senior year rolled around, I was all business. The first game of the year arrived, and I was announced as a defensive player.

Homecoming was about midway through the football season, and I was voted to be part of the Homecoming court. During Homecoming week, the only thing the whole school thinks about is the game on Friday night.

As we were getting ready to take our Homecoming pictures, though, my best friend and I got a call from his dad telling us that our other best friend, Kelly, was involved in a terrible car accident on her way home from school, which had ended in a pep rally that day.

My mom and Kelly's mother, Tammie Foster, were best friends. They were at school because Leslie and Kelly were in the pep rally for Homecoming, and Mom was there to take Homecoming pictures of me. Kelly was driving home after the rally and lunch when the accident happened.

Kelly was Tammie's only daughter. The good that came out of the awful situation was that our families were always there for one another, especially my mom and Tammie, in life and in death.

You can imagine how awful everyone felt to learn this news—that a dear friend was on life support in Macon. We were given the choice to postpone the game, but everyone agreed that we should play this one for Kelly.

We were losing the game at halftime, but we came out and did what we had to do to win the game for Kelly. Everyone went to the hospital after the game to see her. The accident turned out to be fatal for Kelly. So we felt victory and sorrow.

The rest of the year went by very quickly. We made it to the final four after a lot of great football games.

I can't explain to you what it's like—the feeling—when you walk out of the locker room to start warming up and people are already in the stands. When the game starts, and pretty much the whole town is there supporting you, I can't explain the feeling that comes over you. I'm getting chill bumps right now just thinking about it.

During the last game, we were ahead going into the locker room, but we didn't execute during the second half of the game and we ended up losing to the eventual state champions. Still, I was voted an all-region receiver, and we ended up regional champs.

There is nothing like football. My favorite times of high school were most definitely during football season. I had the greatest time of my life during my senior year of high school.

Blake Payne

Blake's teacher commented that the essay seemed a mixture of sorrow and joy—and that Blake had not quite connected how he had the greatest time in football during his senior year and yet suffered the loss of two people. It was a true statement by his teacher, more than he ever knew. He suggested that Blake look deeper into explaining such a profound loss in his life. But at this point Blake was still masking his pain and building walls. Blake only stayed in college at Lee University three weeks until Jacob's birthday on Labor Day. He called and said, "I can't do it. I'm coming home." I tried to talk him out of it, but he had already packed his truck.

Blake still wanted to be Jacob's hero. Football is like life. You put your head down and you fight for inches of ground, against constant obstacles and enemies that are there to keep you from attaining your goal. If you have something to fight for—love—then you do get a victory. I think Blake was feeling all this when he dedicated his season and his year and his game to people who had suffered accidents, and at the same time enjoyed the victories and felt love for them and from the crowds.

After high school Blake worked with his dad in the woods. It can be a very hard time for kids. He had some very angry and depressed times, but he pressed on. We pressed on together. It took years, but God was faithful. Blake's victories were Jacob's victories too. I'm sure Jacob was cheering him on from Heaven. We are, after all, surrounded by a great "cloud of witnesses" of those who have gone before us (Hebrews 12:1). I picture an amphitheatre and an arena—not unlike a football stadium—where we "lay aside every weight, and the sin which so easily ensnares us" and "run with endurance the race that is set before us, looking unto Jesus, the author and finisher of our faith; who for the joy that was set before him endured the cross" (Hebrews 12:1-3).

In that arena we are to be able to say, "I have fought the good fight, I have finished the race, I have kept the faith" (2 Timothy 4:7). We must be able to fight our battles and run our race in front of the great cloud of witnesses that includes all the saints and all those we have loved who have gone to the next world before us and who are cheering for us as we run our courses here on earth.

Our greatest victories can come out of our deepest sorrows.

Chapter Eleven

Longing and Lamentations

Sometimes, in some strange way, I miss those early days of grief. I think it is because I was so close to the Lord, or maybe He was so near to me because I was brokenhearted.

I say that nothing, nothing can compare to my God, Jesus, and the sweet Holy Spirit, the blessed Trinity. How He has been there for me! Although sometimes it was hard to pray, I found Romans 8:26 to be entirely true in my case: "The Spirit also helps us in our weaknesses, for we do not know what we should pray for as we ought, but the Spirit Himself makes intercession for us with groanings which cannot be uttered."

I was very aware of God, but I was also very aware of evil and its presence. In one form or another, the devil and his pack were there, literally trying to devour me and my family. It's hard to fight him, to fight for peace and happiness and renewal in your family and life when you have so little desire even to be on earth anymore. We were mired in battle many times, but we stuck together and came through.

This was a prayer I wrote as our family struggled to work its way through all the stress and strife that Jacob's death had brought upon us. We started going to therapy. Blake would just cry. He could not talk about it.

Prayer

"Lord, right now speak to my children in Your still, small voice that it's okay and we're going to make it. They are in Your hand and so is our family. Show us where to go from here. Give needed rest to us all. Send good times for us to share together and grow stronger. Keep out evil spirits, let peace abound. Help us move on.

"Do a mighty work in us as a whole family and on all sides.

"I'm so proud to be a part of such a special family.

"Good times will come again and blessings. No doubt there will be more death, but be merciful on our broken hearts and give us grace through the moments ahead.

"We are only given one life, which will soon pass.

"Only what is done for Christ will last." That was my grandfather's saying.

I also took comfort from writing in a journal and writing poetry. Here is a poem I wrote about Jacob.

Star of Jacob

Dear God

Thank you for the five years we were
blessed by Jacob's life on earth.

We look forward to eternity together.

Until then we know he is in good hands with
You, Father God, Jesus, and all the saints.

Thank You for the Comforter—the Holy Spirit—which helps
us each day to do Your will and press on without him.

> In eternity, we will be together with
> Mama's precious baby darling
> Leslie's baby, darlin' brother
> Daddy's buddy
> Granny's pumpkin
> Grandmother's angel
> Blake's little brother
> Everybody's baby
> Heaven's Ranger
> Our Angel Ranger.
>
> **Lynn Payne**

Although we all tried to bear up under our loss, the typical strains of life came to us too, particularly as Blake and Leslie grew into their teens. There are normal stresses between teenagers and their parents, but we had the fault line of Jacob's death underneath; our hearts were healing from a major break. Any pressure on this sensitive seam hurt worse than it would have under more normal circumstances.

Sometimes in the eyes of our children, especially when they are teenagers and young adults, we are not seen as who we want to be. They don't see us as we see ourselves, and sometimes they shine a light on us that is not so flattering.

At times when Leslie, my daughter, was a teenager, we had so much friction we could not even be around each other for long without some strain. We'd go from simple chit-chat to a knock-down, drag-out. I know I provoked her at times by being short with her, and she did the same to me.

I had to pray to learn to respect the fact that she was growing up and I shouldn't back her into corners—especially when other people were around.

After a fight, I would feel that we both had lost something. My peace would be gone. It was hard to realize that at those times she perceived me as a negative, mean, insensitive person she didn't want to be around—in other words, a mother.

At the same time, our negative interactions would make me feel like I didn't like myself. I would feel like a failure again, and then I felt accusation about all the mistakes I'd made as a mother over the years. Then I would just want to give up.

Yet when I saw myself as God sees me, I felt like a success. I would look at my children with great pride and feel that they were so great that I must be a good parent. After all, God made me and knows all my weaknesses. He made me a mother. If He finds me worthy, I am worthy, no matter what the devil says.

Although I felt as if it was all I could do to have to breathe each day, we still had to take care of the burdens of everyday life. Without any energy, I still had to cook, clean, shop, plan, pay bills, and go to work every day. Life doesn't stop, even for death. I'm sure everyone else in the family felt the same way, carrying their burdens of lamentations. It made us short with each other many times. The world was not always sensitive to our grief either.

I figured if I walked around wearing black everywhere, even strangers would know I was bereaved, and maybe they would be extra nice and kind to me. But I didn't want everyone to know of my tragedy. It wasn't my total identity; it couldn't be. Although I was a woman who had lost her child, I was much more too. Yet during that time all I felt was that I was a woman bereft of her baby, so it seemed that should be what people saw. I felt black and tainted.

At the same time I wished no one had to see me anyway; I wanted to just stay home where I could nurse my own wounds, but because of Blake and Leslie and Jeff and other family and friends, I couldn't. I would go out for a few hours to take care of doctor's appointments and other necessities, thinking that soon I would be able to retreat again.

I scared myself with this kind of thinking. I scared myself with a lot of things during those confused, grief-saturated days. My mind was so clouded over with sorrow, sometimes I would forget the year and date and month, even though I might have just written it down the day before. I was clinically depressed. I slept whenever possible and couldn't stand being around anybody. The more I slept the more exhausted I became.

I felt sorry that I hadn't appreciated the fact that my life used to be fairly normal and I hadn't even realized how quickly things would change and never be the same. Over and over again, I wondered: "Why did this have to happen to me? Anything would have been easier."

I wondered if I would ever get my strength back. The key seemed to be in my mind, how I thought about things. My thoughts sometimes sapped my strength. Yet I would receive reassurance too.

Thoughts would come to me like: "You are tired. I understand. Accept the covering of Jesus' blood, lest you fall off. The darkness pulls you, but Jesus says it's already over. I have paid the price. You have the strength through Me, your Savior."

In some ways, it was good that everyone still needed me. It's good to be needed. At the same time, I knew I had to spend time with the Lord because I needed Him to take care of me just as my family needed me to take care of them.

I sometimes wondered: "Who takes care of You, Lord?"

The answer came that when we worship God and grow more like Him every day, He feels cared for.

At such moments I knew that I loved God more than anything and that I loved to worship Him. How great are His faithfulness and mercy. Each morning is a new day. I prayed and still pray each day to find peace within the day.

There are times when the words and wisdom in the Bible

just jump out at you and reflect your life as if the pages are alive.
Lamentations (3:19-26) became very familiar to me:

> Remember my affliction and roaming,
> The wormwood and the gall.
> My soul still remembers
> And sinks within me.
> This I recall to my mind,
> Therefore I have hope.
> Through the LORD's mercies we are not consumed,
> Because His compassions fail not.
> They are new every morning;
> Great is Your faithfulness.
> "The LORD *is* my portion," says my soul,
> "Therefore I hope in Him!"
> The LORD is good to those who wait for Him,
> To the soul who seeks Him.
> It is good that one should hope and wait quietly
> For the salvation of the LORD.

I was encouraged also and I could strongly identify with
Lamentations 31-33: "For the Lord will not cast off forever. Though
He causes grief, yet He will show compassion according to the
multitude of His mercies. For He does not afflict willingly, nor
grieve the children of men."

God had given me a deep cup of sorrow to drink, and I will
never forget the awful times as I grieved over my baby. Yet I still
dared to hope when I remembered that great are His faithfulness
and His mercies, starting afresh every day.

"Though He causes grief, yet He will show compassion,
according to the multitude of His mercies" (Lamentations 3:32). I
would repeat this to myself.

Like the writer of Lamentations, I felt like "the waters flowed
over my head; I said, 'I'm cut off!' (3:54) but I called on His name,

from the depths, and He came near when I called Him and said, as He had said in the very first moments when I learned of Jacob's accident: "Do not fear." I could agree heartily with the writer of Lamentations: "Oh, Lord, You have pleaded the case for my soul; You have redeemed my life" (Lamentations 3:58).

Of course, as I've said, day to day life doesn't stop for death. There is still cleaning, cooking, picking up, putting away, washing—so sometimes my prayers were very practical:

"Help me organize! It's so important I stay in control of my house. This has always been hard for me. I just want to get some order. Everything is a mess. This is a sin of waste and I confess. Help me not pass this to my children. My peace of mind depends on things being somewhat normal (as normal as possible)."

Then I would get an inspiration exactly where to start, as if He just opened my eyes and pointed the way, even in such practical things, and I would know what to do and what to do next after that.

I took baby steps toward normalcy. That was all I was able to take in the midst of my lamentations. They were tiny steps, but I was beginning to walk on the path of the rest of my life. I felt like that was what God was doing with me each day, patiently teaching me, and I was slowly learning, in stages, the way I taught Jacob. A parent has to teach a child in little steps.

For example, each morning Jacob used to say to me, "Good morning! Fix my cereal!" I had told Jacob to say "Good morning" first because he'd usually just say, "Fix my cereal," the minute he came downstairs each morning.

He learned to say, "Good morning," pause briefly, and then give his request. Of course, I knew all along what he was up to, and that the "Good morning" was all about him. I still loved him and fixed his cereal because I knew he was going to understand what I was trying to teach him the older he got. I knew he would grow to understand that it is important to acknowledge and appreciate others before yourself. "Good morning" was good enough at first. It was a baby step toward that lifelong journey of learning to see others as God sees them—as precious and important in their own rights.

As God taught me, He became my closest friend. He understood me like no one else. Just as a mother knows her children and helps them over all their little hills, faults, and lapses so that they can grow to be good people, the Lord helps us become the people He wants us to be.

Chapter Twelve

Defeat and Victory— "Battle Born"

Healing was hard. This is a journal entry I made a little over a half a year after Jacob's death:

"It's been a long time; almost seven months, but it still feels so much like I'm living in a fog. I should be feeling better, but the reality of what has happened keeps hitting. Everyone is still nice to me, but it's really just my family and You who know my constant state of sorrow. You know everything about me; You can even read my mind. The sorrow never stops. Sometimes I just want to scream, 'Stop! Stop!' When I sleep, dreams come and I can't begin to say how strange and tormented they are. Each night is a struggle."

In fact, I dreamed many nights about a boardwalk past the local pond and train tracks near Galamore Road. In the dream, I was rushing frantically to gather my loved ones. It was dark and time was short, and I was so worried.

I had this dream on and off for decades. Sometimes when I ride through the area in waking life, I wonder and worry about its meaning.

The boardwalk in my dreams is a very busy place, and it

reminds me of the Bible verse Matthew 7:13 -14: "Enter through the narrow gate; for wide is the gate and broad is the road that leads to destruction, and many enter through it. But small is the gate and narrow the road that leads to life, and only a few find it." The boardwalk is not of importance; it is the gate that is important, and in my dreams I desperately want to find it. I cannot see the end of the boardwalk; it just disappears into the woods. It seems as if one would just drop off into utter darkness.

So many are moving on the bridge or boardwalk, but the important thing is to find the narrow gate. The narrow gate in my dreams is, I believe, the gateway to eternal life through salvation. It takes faith to step out of the natural into the supernatural, out of this life into the next. We need Jesus as our conductor, or it is all dark, scary, and a difficult passageway. He is the gateway. Yet in our busyness, we often don't find the gateway, and then we are in a scary place.

Please do not neglect the salvation that is offered. It will be a great comfort to you, and it will help you find meaning in your loss. Hebrews 2:1-4 says: "How shall we escape if we neglect so great a salvation, which at the first began to be spoken by the Lord, and was confirmed to us by those who heard Him; God also bearing witness both with signs and wonders, with various miracles, and gifts of the Holy Spirit, according to His own will?"

When I prayed that my dreams would get better, they did.

"It will be eight months soon, and I still haven't taken the pictures and his letters that he got for Christmas and his name JACOB off the refrigerator. I think there's still some food in the freezer people brought at the time, and his clothes are still in the laundry room: pjs, underwear, and play clothes I kept down there for convenience. Sometimes when I drop something, when I lean down or walk in, if I look just right, I see his clothes, since the drawers are clear. His red and polka dot colored pjs jump out at me like a ghost. The knife turns again in my heart. I still have moments when I just can't believe it—he has been, then gone, like a dream.

"His birthday is in a few weeks. Some people have offered to help get together his baby book, to help organize the pictures, et cetera. I made this my goal months back. Help me to pull everything together and even deal with some of his clothes while I have help. I'll never forget him, but I think it will help to get things in order—after all, he is not coming back. But I've got to stay here and stay with the peace I know You'll give me in time."

Looking for ways to honor Jacob and to keep giving to him, I planned a party for his birthday. It was just family. I honored him by displaying pictures of him, and I gave everyone presents and some pictures to remember him. Jeff and I both thanked everyone for coming, and I testified to them that I just wanted to be happy again to bring glory to God somehow through the tragedy.

As early as 2004, I was able to give some testimony to the Lord. On October 3rd, a Sunday night, I had my first chance to testify. It was in front of some ladies from our church—perhaps twenty to thirty ladies at our church. A little healing had taken place; I was able to say that God was seeing me through in a miraculous way, and that I could see His hand everywhere. My main concern in giving the testimony was that I hoped people could feel my heart rather than that I would be eloquent. That was what mattered to me.

I learned through my loss and grief that I am His masterpiece, made of clay, holding the power of the Holy Spirit, so together we can bring light into the darkness of grief. Jesus was a man of sorrows and well-acquainted with grief. Yet He is the light of the world. Surely He has borne our griefs and carried our sorrows. He will show us the way out and through.

In some ways, too, if you are a believer, you were chosen to grieve and experience losses, the same way any warrior experiences some losses. You can lose battles and still win the war. It's a rare warrior who wins both the war and every single battle.

If you are a believer, you were battle born, for we live in a world that is broken, a world full of sin, and a world where things are far from perfect. If you have given your life over to God, it's going to be a battle. You are going to be on the front lines, and it is inevitable that you are going to lose some battles and experience grief. As Christians, we will lose many battles and comrades even as we win the war that Jesus already won.

Do not be afraid because no matter how the battle ends, we are destined to win.

BATTLE BORN

Born for battle I hear You say

The thought of another, I can't even pray

Still bruised from previous ones, I am battle worn

My heart is heavy I want to run

Close the curtain: THE END

I wouldn't know where to begin

You say it's not up to me, I am a soldier in Your army

In my flesh, I am torn

Again You whisper: "Battle born."

You hand me Your mighty weapons of warfare for breaking

strongholds and the thoughts and doubts in my own head

On my frail body Your armor You place,

Covered with blood and covered with grace

"This is the blood of My Son.

The day you accepted Him you were battle born."

Lynn Payne

He is saying also to you who are spiritually worn out and feel as if you were left for dead, "I will breathe My Spirit into you. Rise up, My great army, you who have been slain and live again, for you are battle born."

As I've mentioned, life does not stop because a loss has occurred. You have to go about your business—suffering a tragedy does not automatically mean you will not suffer in your relationships, your finances, your health, or in other ways. You would think we would be exempt from suffering after a heavy loss, but that is not the case. Life goes on, with all its challenges.

By the time a decade had come and gone since Jacob's death, I was able to bring glory to God in my own way. Here is a poem written a decade after that first, halting testimony to the ladies of my church. It was a poetic time for me. I think you can feel the gathering strength in me; the new storehouses of peace and reconciliation in my soul as God renewed and restored me—a sense of victory and joy.

October 30, 2014
Feast in the Famine

Here I am again Lord
My soul is in a famine
Jehovah Nissi, Your banner over me
I am in a famine of the spirit
Looking to you, Yahweh God
I recall past seasons of restoration
Still, I feel an undeniable chill inside
Spirit of heaviness sweeping through me
Rebuking anxious thoughts, I release a praise
Icy trees crashing down like the walls around me

In my own strength, I am bankrupt

Seek first the kingdom and all these things shall be added

Walking the tightrope of pride and perfection (I am falling)

Falling into the net of Your grace

In humility, I can see depending on You and not on me

I surrender my limitations and insecurities to You

You remove my mask of perfection

You say it is my weakness that reveals Your reflection

You place on me a robe of Your righteousness

You take me through doors to which only You have the key

It is the storehouses of Heaven, tables set for me

It is more than my mind can conceive:
peace, joy, love, and family

A feast in the famine, You are all I see

You restore my soul, my cup runneth over

As You wave Your banner of love and victory over me!

Lynn Payne

That is not to say that things were easy—they were just easier, and a lot of light had broken through the darkness. Most of all, I had learned that the less there was of me, the more there was of God. My poems reflected that.

They also reflect the chill of winter that still shows through some in my poems. Perhaps that is so because it is the season in which Jacob died. I was marked by what had happened, and I never would be unmarked again.

October 30, 2014

Fields of Favor

Here I am again, Lord
You've got my attention, I am in a famine
Is that why You stop the rain?
Here I am again, Lord.
The seasons change
Jehovah Jirah, my needs You provide
Looking to You, Yahweh God
I recall past seasons You've already brought me through
Yet today there is a chill in the air
Bringing fear of winter to my mind
So many questions and concerns (for today and tomorrow)
It is time for dead things to fall off (like the leaves on the trees)
In my own strength, I came up short
Your word says You give me the power to get wealth
In humility, I can see depending on You and not on me
Pride has to end, no peace to be found
Bigger, better, looking all around
Only You can fill that space inside of me
Breaking strongholds I surrender to You
My limitations and lack that overwhelm me
You take my hand, now Your glory can shine through
You lead me to fields of favor.
You show me seeds I have sown

As I reap the harvest of this dark season,
lessons from winter I will glean
It is truly better to give than receive
Blessed to be a blessing, that is Your will for me!

Lynn Payne

The only way I was able to get through was through giving myself more and more over to God. That was when peace began, and I could praise God. What was the beginning of a turnaround, a decade after the loss, is really beginning to take flight in this praise poem I wrote a year later:

June 17, 2015

Jesus, You Are . . .
The Dream Giver
The Heart Healer
The Peace Keeper
The Joy Restorer
The Shepherd King
My soul will sing, You are amazing
In Your name I find everything
You are gentle like a Lamb
Fierce as a Lioness, sweeping me from my enemy
Destroying thoughts warring against me
A daughter of the King, I am royalty

A son of the King a Prince You will be
The Lion is the Lamb, it's not just an analogy
In Heaven our future is secure
If on Earth our trials we endure
No more walking through Death's Valley
Man's fallen nature will be restored
Every tear wiped away, hurts remembered no more
Never again to feel alone, Heaven will be our eternal home
Many loved ones you will see, making up for lost time
What a day that will be!
Jesus, You are . . .
The Door to Peace Forevermore.

Lynn Payne

I had found, from the first, that giving myself over to the Holy Spirit had kept me going through those first frightening hours and days, and it continued to buoy me up throughout the years:

September 14, 2014
Good Morning, Holy Spirit
Holy Spirit, fall on me
Holy Spirit, who do You want me to be
Shine Your light and help me see
Holy Spirit, flow through me
Share Your wisdom

In You, I can be Holy

Holy Spirit, You comfort me

Blessed Trinity #3

It is You I never want to grieve

By my actions and the words I speak

I pray You never leave

Make Your home inside of me

I'm not strong enough

Yet in You all things I can do

I can't live if living is without You!

Lynn Payne

Over time, I felt less and less like an exile on this earth and more like someone who had a special connection with eternity. Of course, my baby was there, with Jesus—and that helped me separate from worldly things and put God first.

We are just sojourners here, finding our way home to God. As time went on my surety and certainty in God's love and purpose for me grew. My poems turned from lamentations into pure praise.

I hope you can sense, especially in the last poem, how peaceful, how reconciled and worshipful to God I became. After a decade, the sorrow and loss had been transformed into heart-throbbing love for God and a distinct sense of victory.

This is not just a book to me. It is a labor of love. But it has been so hard. Even as I write it, I wonder how I will finish it, and doubts creep in, but I am aware of some urgency behind it. God has been showing me a lot. I try to be His servant. I was not an eyewitness of Jesus' life and am even less worthy because of my comfortable life. Yet somehow, I feel like a beloved disciple because Jesus makes me feel that way. He teaches us, cares for us, loves us. Oh, how He loves us. I hope He can work his plan through me because I try to be a willing vessel.

Tweet 1/12/13:

In my weakness I shall boast though they overwhelm me. You are my strength. You worked Your plan through me because I am Your willing vessel!

We must not fear. We must claim the promise of God in 2 Timothy 1:7: "For God has not given us a spirit of fear, but of power and of love and of a sound mind." If we suffer, we are partakers "of the suffering of the gospel according to the power of God" (2 Timothy 1:8). We are called "with a holy calling, not because of our works, but according to His own purpose and grace which was given to us in Christ Jesus" (2 Timothy 1:9).

We can do all things through Christ who strengthens us. There comes that vital moment when we turn to God and say, "You must do this, Lord. I can't," as C. S. Lewis said. We strive to keep our eyes on God and His perfect plan, knowing that when we don't know what we are doing, He does. When we don't have the strength, He will give it to us. *He will equip us and anoint us to accomplish what He desires. We must not fear. He will send the resources. Do not worry. Do not hold on to control.*

Tweet: 8/23/17:

When God ignites a passion in you to accomplish a thing, it is His purpose that prevails. You can persevere in His strength until completion.

There is a purpose to our suffering. Pastor Rick Warren of Saddleback Church, who lost his own son to suicide, said that the final stage of grieving is service. We turn our suffering into service, so that our victories can help others get theirs.

I have learned a lot about grief, both from God and from counselors and from working it out and crying it out myself. I hope to share some of that with those who are experiencing sorrow, so as to give them a lift on their paths as they walk a way with me on mine.

We've all heard a lot about the five stages of grief over a loss. Elisabeth Kübler-Ross discovered these five stages through her work with dying patients. She found that those who suffer a serious loss of health that was leading to death—people facing the loss of their lives to diseases like cancer—go through five stages: 1.) denial/shock 2.) anger 3.) bargaining 4.) depression or sadness, and finally, 5.) acceptance and peace.

Kübler-Ross's five stages have been argued over by some experts, and no one who has ever experienced a loss would say that the stages march neatly right in a row until one day acceptance comes, and the person is able to move on. Some people don't feel any anger; some people never get to acceptance and peace but are bitter and cynical all the rest of their lives. For others, even after acceptance, that old sense of shock and denial crops up again sometimes: "Did that really happen? Wasn't it all a bad dream? Could I really have had such a loss in my life? Is there any way to go back, even now, and change the past so that the terrible thing didn't happen? Please, can I have a do-over?"

I felt all these things at different times, and sometimes all of them at the same time. The grieving person should not judge himself or herself when going through these different phases of coping with loss, even when he or she seems to go back into a stage that "should" be over, like the initial denial or shock stage. Grief is a little like a trampoline—there are ups and downs, backs and forths, times when you sink below the level of the surface and other times when you spring up quite high.

All the time your heart is being stretched and refashioned into something more beautiful and refined. The process hurts very badly, but there will be a worthwhile result.

With even the greatest of griefs, we have to learn to rely on God's promises. He says He can make all things new again: in Revelation 21:5, it says: "And he that sat upon the throne said, 'Behold, I make all things new.'" You can have a new life, new dreams, new hopes, and fresh happiness even after the most grievous of losses.

God has also promised that He will dry every tear. He promised this again and again, in both the Old and the New Testaments.

In Isaiah 25:8, it says: "He will swallow up death in victory, and the Lord God will wipe away tears from off all faces."

In Revelation 7:17, it says, "For the Lamb which is in the midst of the throne shall feed them, and shall lead them unto living fountains of waters: and God shall wipe away all tears from their eyes."

Then in Revelation 21:4, it says, "And God shall wipe away all tears from their eyes, and there shall be no more death, neither sorrow, nor crying, neither shall there be any more pain, for the former things have passed away."

Sometimes we may think that our troubles and sorrows are too great to be healed or mended, but that means we are underestimating God. He can even cause water to flow in a desert.

Isaiah 35:6 says, "Then shall the lame man leap as an hart, and the tongue of the dumb sing, for in the wilderness shall waters break out, and streams in the desert."

The nation of Israel is a desert place, yet it is full of fruits, flowers, and wonderful crops because God wrought the miracle of making streams in the desert. If God can do that to a place on earth, surely He can do it inside the human heart. He can bring waters of grace and rivulets of healing to the desert-like, rock-hard soil of a broken and defeated soul.

There will be setbacks, of course. Lately I have been convicted of how I have sometimes mumbled and complained to myself, maybe not so much by my physical words but by the expressions on my face. You can't hide it when you are feeling defeated.

But I'm not defeated. I just am a saint who has fallen down. I fall down many times, but I always try to get up again, with God's help. Here is my confession:

Confessions

I'm coming back to your heart (My first Love)
I've been in a fog, can't see you (My vision)
I can feel you, but I can't touch you (My hands)
You pull me out of the darkness (My Eyes)
I'm tired of letting you down (My Father)
I feel like I'm just taking up space (My Life)
I want to see you in my dreams again (My Destiny)
Eating apples we were never meant to (The Fall)
Choking the life out of who I am supposed to be (My Call)
But it's not hopeless, that's why Jesus came (My Savior)
You are faithful; not me, I am weak (My strength)
Restore to me the fellowship we once shared (My friend)
Create in me a new heart and forgive my sin (My Joy).

Lynn Payne

Chapter Thirteen

Life with a Purpose

Somehow you have to find the will to go on, and that comes from finding your purpose. That purpose will sustain you, because people's hearts can turn a little callous toward you sooner than you would think after a tragic loss. They want to go about their business and they expect you to go about yours. I'm not sure that they realize that the wounds never completely go away.

I wrote a poem about that:

> When people hurt my feelings
> I wish they wouldn't
> Believe me, it's not hard
> You thought I should be over my grieving
> But I'm tainted, forever scarred
> See, I've always been tender-hearted.
> Even if I deserved a stern word
> Can't they see how fragile my heart is
> I cry and I cry at the least unkind word

Even a mean look is like a knife in my chest

Maybe I imagined it; I am at such unrest

When people hurt my feelings

Why, why? I cry.

I am just doing my best

Did they forget my loss?

I'm sorry their empathy didn't last

I guess my pain doesn't give me a pass

A little more grace: Is that too much to ask?

I know they have struggles of their own

I really just wish you had never gone

How dare they forget; I can never forget

I guess they didn't know I'll always be grieving

When people hurt my feelings

I wish they wouldn't.

Lynn Payne

I sometimes think of Jesus when James and John, the sons of Zebedee, came to him and said, "Teacher, we want You to do for us whatever we ask" (Mark 10:35) and it turned out that what they desired was to sit at His right hand and at His left hand in Heaven and in glory. Jesus said to them that they did not know what they were asking for, and if they wanted that, they had to be ready to drink the bitter cup He had to drink from (Mark 10:38). If they wanted the glory, were they willing to partake of the sorrow and the suffering?

Some, a few I know, have drunk from the cup of sorrow that I have. Yet most have not. When they say things that hurt me, I wish they could know my sorrow. Not that I am wishing it upon them, but that they could know that the course I have walked has not been easy.

Sometimes in our relationship with God and Jesus, even if we are following as closely as we can, we will fall head first into a pit of suffering. Maybe we will even be pushed into it, like Joseph was thrown into a pit by his jealous brothers. Maybe we will be thrown into the fire of punishment like Shadrach, Meshach, and Abednego. Certainly David spoke of being in a miry pit.

We can entrust our lives into His hands even in such a situation. Our bodies may get hurt; we may not even survive. Yet our souls are in His hands, and our souls are His concern. We may have never dreamed such a thing would interrupt our usual lives, but it did and other things may do so too.

We may even be hung upside down like Peter was hung. Peter too had hoped for a lovely kingdom here on earth, one of glamor and beauty. Don't we all? Yet, like Peter with his misplaced but beautiful passion, we are not always given what we want and expect. I'm sure Peter's heart broke when Jesus died, but the Holy Spirit brought all the words Jesus had spoken to him back to him, and Peter too accepted his cross with humility. His ministry exploded after Jesus' death, and he lived his destiny well and made Jesus proud. Jesus gave Peter the power to preach Pentecost and to do many miracles. Even with a broken heart, Peter changed the world with the power that worked through him.

I think of another old song, some of the words of which are: "To be like Jesus, to be like Jesus, that's all I ask, to be like Him all through life's journey from Earth to Glory." We sing songs like this, and yet we forget how Jesus suffered. If we want the glory and to be like him, we too must take up our crosses. In Matthew 16:24, it says: "Then Jesus said unto his disciples, 'If any man will come after me, let him deny himself, and take up his cross, and follow me." Jesus goes on to say: "For whoever desires to save his life shall lose it, but whoever loses his life for My sake will find it" (Matthew

16:25). It doesn't matter if we gain the whole world if we lose our souls (Matthew 16:26).

We must walk after the Spirit, not the flesh (Romans 8:4-9). That means life on this earth may not be easy. That means we may lose our lives; we may lose our livelihoods; we may lose our well-being and all that is precious to us and that makes for earthly happiness. Yet if we lose our lives for this earth, we gain our lives for Heaven (Luke 9:24).

These are not easy things to know or say. All that can be said is that if we drink the cup of sorrow on earth, if we fall into a miry pit, if we must take up a painful cross and bear it, then our minds turn more to the life of the spirit than to the flesh. We fasten our gaze on Heaven and put our faith there. "You have been grieved by various trials, that the genuineness of your faith, being much more precious than gold that perishes, though it is tested by fire, may be found to praise, honor, and glory at the revelation of Jesus Christ"(1 Peter 1:6-7).

I have always been a worshipper. The day came when I danced in praise of the Lord again, in public, at church. I had always done this kind of worship, but I had become still for so long. It was not a planned testimony of dance worship, but now I realize that's what took place.

I told the Lord: "Every day we dance to the music of the day, and sometimes I get out of step with You. However, You are a patient teacher, and I hope one day You can say that I was a good student."

I praised and I wrote poems to the Lord.

Chasing After You

I am chasing after You
Setting my mind on things of the Spirit

I want to please You . . . praise is what I do
I give myself away
If I am ruled by my sinful self
I cannot please You; I must give myself away
In order to gain my life, I must lose it,
Take up my cross, deny myself and follow You
These words to Your beloved You said
"Whoever loses his life for Me will save it.
What profit a man if he gains the whole world to lose his soul?"

Lynn Payne

I try to be like Jesus, passing through the hard times and bearing my cross with God's strength and through the Holy Spirit who abides in me. Few may know or understand my pain, but as long as God is here, I'm okay.

I have come to find a purpose in my pain, and that purpose is to help others who are suffering a loss and who are in pain and confusion because of that loss.

This book is part of that. I've been asked what I wish to accomplish with this book. My answer has always been to help others who are hurting desperately and give them the one tool that can help overcome any obstacle: the Gospel of Jesus Christ.

I promise those of you who are suffering losses, there is comfort over time. There is even joy. God has promised to turn our mourning into dancing if we just persevere in praise. In the kingdom of God, we advance beyond our sorrow and grief when we praise God. As I praise Him through this trial and the many more to come, I am humbled and a miracle is being birthed. In my weakness, His strength and His power are made perfect.

The time came when I gathered up all my grief books to give to the church library so they could be of help to someone else who was suffering a loss. I pondered what to write inside. The only words I could think of to write on the inside were, "May God help you," the same words I wrote in a card to someone who had just lost his daughter. God is the biggest help when you are coping with a loss.

Though I had my doubts that He would see me through, He did. I have realized that I will make it, but only with God's help. I can say boldly God will help you because He has helped me.

Our Father which art in Heaven

I will honor you as long as I live.

My thirsty soul

Is satisfied in You.

I lie awake thinking of You.

You protect me

You are holding me

Greater love than life

Sanctuary

Day after day, night after night

I will honor You

I will praise Your name with my hands

I am satisfied in You

> Satisfied—a word for my spirit and my life with You.
>
> If I never have a blessed day again, I am satisfied in You.
>
> **Lynn Payne**

Life went on, and I worked as the receptionist at the same office for my brother's timber company until 2011. The last few years I have owned a tea shop and now do catering for small events. As I serve others in my calling, I strive to become more like Jesus. I use my gift of hospitality, which I received from my mother, and I use my passion for people and God's Word, which I received from my father, in order to accomplish my destiny.

I am thankful that I have healed and now have love in my heart for youths. I enjoyed years of teaching Sunday School to the teens at our home church that my daddy started in Jeffersonville. We have attended church in Macon at Real Life Church the past five years or more, which we consider home also. God led us there, and I've worked with the youth a few years now; it is such an amazing ministry. I always believed God would give me a large family as a blessing for all we went through. Again I see this manifested by all the children I love and mentor in this ministry, which I consider my family. I also work in areas of hospitality in the church, which is also a testimony to how God has helped me, because for so many years I avoided parties and happy celebrations. I have tried to help many grieving people through the years, and I am excited to walk in my call however the Lord opens the doors through this book.

My father, William Stuckey Shepherd "Bill," passed away as I was writing this book. He is truly the reason I am strong enough in my faith to finish it. I have fought many spirits that were against this book, and my flesh was my worst enemy. My flesh doesn't like discipline, but the Spirit which lives in me is stronger. This thorn in my flesh, which actually is my flesh, will not win because God's

Word says "My Grace is sufficient for you; my spirit is made perfect in weakness." I can testify to that.

As I have said, I have come to trust God with my most profound loss and to embrace my destiny. I have found purpose in my pain and will turn it into a blessing for others.

My Destiny

Before I was born, You had a plan for me
Everything lined up quite strategically
My house of flesh is the thorn You gave
All the pain, manipulation, and evil You see
See my unfair treatment and forgive my iniquity
My motive is pure and my mandate from You
My face is brighter now, wiser than before
I thought my life was over ... joy no more
Even though my heart was broken by You
The gift of Your spirit was given too
As You restore, I am better than before
In death, a dream was birthed only You could see
Like the seeds beneath Winter bursting forth in Spring
From the ashes blooms my heart with praises to You
Blocking the anxious thoughts from my enemy
You tell me to write my destiny
By Your Spirit, I am transformed
I can do this thing ... It is why I was born.

I know I will confess with the Lord's help in His perfect time. I have thought of starting a children's charity in Jacob's name.

Many will be blessed and much good will be done because of Jacob Karl Payne's life.

Epilogue

There comes time and a season for everything, as Ecclesiastes 3 reminds us; There is "A time to weep, and a time to laugh; a time to mourn, and a time to dance." (Ecclesiastes 3:4).

The time will come if it hasn't already, when You are ready to stop mourning Your loss and spending Your days in grief. There will be a time to laugh, to dance, and experience joy again.

As we weep with Rachel over our losses, we cannot refuse to be comforted. We must accept the Comforted and grow and heal through our painful times.

Jacob, Rachel's husband refused to be comforted over a lie that was causing him grief. Jacob's son Joseph, was his favorite. Joseph's brothers cast him into a pit and then sold him into slavery in Egypt and decided to tell their father, Jacob, that Joseph had been killed by wild animals. When Jacob heard this about his favorite son, he refused to be comforted.

"Then Jacob tore his clothes, put sackcloth on his waist, mourned for his son many days. And all his son's and all his daughters arose to comfort him, but he refused to be comforted; and he said 'For I will go down into the grave to my son in mourning. 'Thus his father wept for him. (Genesis 37:34-35) ,

Jacob's grief was spent on a lie: Joseph was alive and he became Prime minister of Egypt. Later on He saved his whole family from famine, and was reunited with his father, who had grieved hard and long over his loss. Because of Joseph's position He had a chance to mistreat or even take revenge on his brothers. But He had come to the place in his journey of healing that He realized God had worked all these things together for good. He was walking out his destiny and the dream the Lord has given him as a boy. His season of pain had passed and his season of purpose had come.

The time comes when the Lord says to us: Refrain your voice from weeping and your eyes from tears; for your work shall be rewarded , says the Lord , and they shall come back from the land of the enemy" (Jeremiah 31:16)

In our losses no matter how genuine let us not believe the lie from the enemy that we will never be blessed again and that our lives can never be restored. You must keep faith in God and be comforted by the Holy Spirit. I pray You accept his healing comfort and in God's perfect time you will also enter into your season of purpose. I want to be better because of the life of my son Jacob Karl Payne. His life was not in vain. I love You forever my son.

JACOB'S FAMILY PHOTO ALBUM

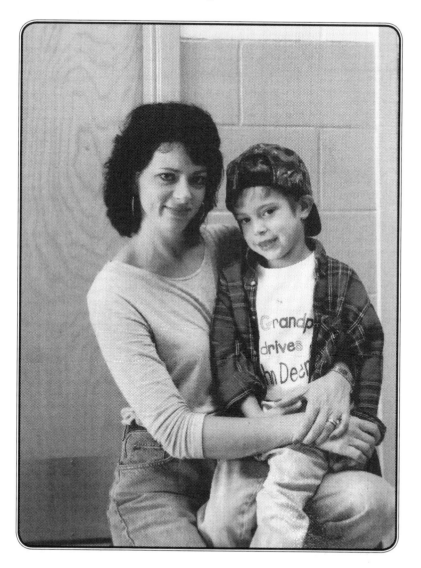

JACOB

FE IN JESUS' LOVING ARMS

JACOB KARL PAYNE
SEPT. 8, 1997
DEC. 27, 2002

Granddaughter Anslee Blaire Payne Born 12/13 /11